# THE LORD KNEADS YOU

## YOU

A Companion to

## DARE TO PREPARE

*BEST WISHES AND WORK HARD !*

*[signature]*

# THE LORD
# KNEADS
# YOU

A Companion to
## DARE TO PREPARE

by
Lyman Hinckley Rose

**BONNEVILLE BOOKS**™
Springville, Utah

ISBN: 1-55517-727-1
e. 1

Published by Bonneville Books
Imprint of Cedar Fort Inc.
www.cedarfort.com

Distributed by:

Typeset by Natalie K. Roach
Cover design by Nicole Cunningham
Cover design © 2003 by Lyle Mortimer

Printed in the United States of America
10 9 8 7 6 5 4 3 2 1

Printed on acid-free paper

Library of Congress Control Number: 2003098312

# DEDICATION

Once again, I would like to dedicate this work to every missionary who has shown the courage to go out into the world and preach the living gospel.

# ACKNOWLEDGMENTS

I would like to again acknowledge Loren C. Dunn and Orson Wright who tirelessly served as my mission presidents.

I would also like to acknowledge my family for allowing me the time to spend on this project.

Finally, I would like to acknowledge the missionaries who are serving and who are preparing to serve for their dedication and great efforts. It is for them that this work is written.

# TABLE OF CONTENTS

# INTRODUCTION

Hopefully you have read the book *Dare to Prepare*. That book covered several of the concepts that I teach to missionaries who are preparing to go out into the field. Each chapter of the book has an assignment at the end and I encouraged the readers to fulfill each of the assignments. This book is in the same format with end-of-chapter assignments. It is a continuation of the lesson material that I teach to young men and women who are preparing to serve the Lord in the mission field. It is not necessary that you have read *Dare to Prepare* before you read this book but it is highly recommended that you read them both.

You certainly are a chosen generation and a blessed people to have the gospel in its fullness and to be selected to share it throughout the world. I am sure that you realize that the adversary is aware of your special talents and he has probably made himself manifest in various ways in his attempt to derail you from your eternal course. Now that's a long sentence that simply means Satan has sorely tempted you because he knows who you are.

So who is going to win? The more you try to live the gospel, the more the adversary tries to turn you away. Just the fact that he pays so much attention to you should tell you how special you are! He will continue to put on the pressure until, like Moroni, you reach the state where he has no power over you. "Yea, verily, verily I say unto you, if all men had been, and were, and ever would be, like unto Moroni, behold, the very powers of hell would have been shaken forever, yea, the devil would never have power over the hearts of the children of men" (Alma

48:17). But until we reach that state of heart and mind and spirit, we must constantly be on the watch for the things that he is doing to try to get us out of the race.

Know that you are chosen and set apart for this great work in these latter days. Your foreordination was probably very clear on the subject of serving a mission. Don't waste that great blessing!

Now let's get to work and see just how prepared you can be when you enter the mission field. In this book we will go over principles that will have the potential to prepare you for many of the experiences you will have while in the field. They will also supply you with information that will strengthen your testimony and give you an understanding of the power of God in His work. The adversary may be strong but God is far stronger and can sustain you through anything.

If you will complete the assignments at the end of the chapters, you will receive a great deal more out of this book than if you don't. The difference would be equivalent to watching someone ride a roller coaster or being in the front car. There is no work nearly as exciting as missionary work in all of the worlds Father has created! Just make up your mind that you will do the assignments as you go and you will feel much better when you are finished.

The title of the book is more than a mere play on words. The Lord really does need you and the Lord really does knead you. He needs you to do this work and to stand in His shoes as though they were your own. He needs you to be an instrument in blessing the lives of countless numbers of your brothers and sisters. He needs you to lead in the work and in the church. The Lord also kneads you by helping you to learn the principles that will change your life. He kneads you through reproof and correction. He kneads you by giving you problems to overcome to strengthen you. He will knead you into the shape and form of His own image if you will, in humility, let Him. He can only knead you if you let Him and if you keep yourself pliable enough for His tender hands to mold you into a perfected son or daughter.

Now move forward and don't turn back! Let your missionary experience be a blessing to your entire life both here and throughout eternity.

# ITEMS TO COMMIT TO MEMORY

At the beginning of every class, we stand together and repeat the following four items:  D&C Section 4, 3 Nephi 5:13, Mormon 9:21 and The Standard of Truth. I will reproduce all of them here so you can begin to memorize them all and repeat them every day to yourself or others. The message they carry is extremely powerful.

### *Doctrine and Covenants Section 4*

1 NOW behold, a marvelous work is about to come forth among the children of men.
2 Therefore, O ye that embark in the service of God, see that ye serve him with all your heart, might, mind and strength, that ye may stand blameless before God at the last day.
3 Therefore, if ye have desires to serve God ye are called to the work;
4 For behold the field is white already to harvest; and lo, he that thrusteth in his sickle with his might, the same layeth up in store that he perisheth not, but bringeth salvation to his soul;
5 And faith, hope, charity and love, with an eye single to the glory of God, qualify him for the work.
6 Remember faith, virtue, knowledge, temperance, patience, brotherly kindness, godliness, charity, humility, diligence.
7 Ask, and ye shall receive; knock, and it shall be opened unto you. Amen.

### 3 Nephi 5:13

Behold, I am a disciple of Jesus Christ, the Son of God. I have been called of him to declare his word among his people, that they might have everlasting life.

### Mormon 9:21

Behold, I say unto you that whoso believeth in Christ, doubting nothing, whatsoever he shall ask the Father in the name of Christ it shall be granted him; and this promise is unto all, even unto the ends of the earth.

### The Standard of Truth - Joseph Smith Jr.

The Standard of Truth has been erected; no unhallowed hand can stop the work from progressing; persecutions may rage, mobs may combine, armies may assemble, calumny may defame, but the truth of God will go forth boldly, nobly, and independent, till it has penetrated every continent, visited every clime, swept every country, and sounded in every ear, till the purposes of God shall be accomplished, and the Great Jehovah shall say the work is done [HC 4:540].

# CHAPTER 1

# OPPOSITION: HOW CAN I ENDURE AND ENDURE WELL?

Let's start off with an experiment. Find a very small rock or pebble about the size of a pea. Then find also a piece of candy. Put the candy in your mouth and the pebble in your shoe right under the middle of your foot so you can feel it very well when you stand up. Now I want you to take a walk around your house or to the park, somewhere outside. I want you to walk for about five or ten minutes and then return back to the book. Go ahead. Do it! Don't go on until you have done it. I promise I'll be right here when you get back!

I hope you just returned from your walk and are not just continuing to read. Now, get out a small piece of paper and write about your experience using one single word. No cheating, use only one word. Now in my class, I gather the papers and write the responses on the board. About 95 percent of the time they say things like 'exasperating,' 'irritating,' 'annoying,' 'uncomfortable,' 'pain,' 'hurt,' and 'ouch' (probably the most frequent word). What did you write? Was it something similar? Now I ask you, (assuming that your response was somewhat similar to 95 percent of what I see) what about the piece of candy? Why didn't you use the word 'sweet' or 'yummy' or 'delicious' to describe your experience? If you went out in the evening, were there stars in the sky or was there a beautiful sunset? If in the morning, was there a sunrise or a bird singing? Were there beautiful clouds and a refreshing rain or was the sky blue and warm? Was there a cool breeze or some silent snowflakes gently falling to touch the earth? Wasn't there at least one thing that was beautiful about your walk? I'm sure there must have been something. Why didn't you mention that in your one word synopsis of your walk?

It always amazes me that as humans we tend to focus on the negative no matter how small. The piece of candy was probably bigger than the pebble (there aren't many pieces of candy that are smaller than a pea) yet the focus was on the negative impact of the pebble. Compare the size and weight of the pebble with you own size and weight. How many thousands of times bigger are you than that little bothersome pebble? When we focus on the negative, we lose sight of the positive. All of the beautiful and sweet things in life seem to disappear because we are concentrating on the negative.

(If you wrote something positive in your one word description, I apologize for taking you to task on this.)

As we just mentioned above in the introduction to the book, you will see opposition in your work and you may see it from several sources. You might see it from the people you have been called to teach and you might also see it from your companion. We will examine both of these sources and see if we can't find a way to deal with it.

First, let's look at the opposition you may receive from the people where you serve. One very important fact to remember when receiving opposition from the people is that they don't oppose you, they oppose what they perceive your message to be. It's almost impossible for them to dislike you because they don't usually know you at all! Once they get to know you, then they can despise you, but not until then. (Of course they will love you when they get to know who you are and what you are bringing to them.)

Normally the opposition you receive from the people is in the form of rejection—a turned back, a slammed door or simply saying, "I'm not interested." Don't let it get to you! You are a disciple of Jesus Christ and you have been called by Him to declare His word among His people so that they might receive eternal life (See 3 Nephi 5:13).

Occasionally you might run into someone who feels the need to express their hostility in a more forceful manner. When my companion and I were tracting in a large apartment building, a group of young men destroyed our bikes while we were in the building and later threw fruit and eggs at us from the top of the 26 floor structure. If they had hit us, it would have done some real damage. If you come across someone like this, just remember that you have the favor of Ahman (God) and you can endure this world's bitter hate (See Hymns "The Time is Far Spent"). Opposition of this harsher kind is normally infrequent. Some missionaries never do experience it.

Once again remember that they are rejecting your message, not you. Also remember that the only reason they are rejecting your message is because they simply don't understand it. If the really did, they would line up at the baptismal font.

When the Lord gave the Sermon on the Mount He said "Blessed are they which are persecuted for righteousness' sake: for theirs is the kingdom of heaven. Blessed are ye, when men shall revile you, and persecute you, and shall say all manner of evil against you falsely, for my sake. Rejoice, and be exceeding glad: for great is your reward in heaven: for so persecuted they the prophets which were before you" (Matt 5:10-12).

Although it is difficult to deal with rejection and persecution, the promise of the Lord is that you will receive a great reward in heaven. What that reward is or when we will receive it is of little importance. The fact that God promised it is our assurance that it will come to pass.

The more we learn to love the people the more we become tolerant of their negative treatment of us. Our love for the people turns our anger into a desire to help and a pity for their foundationless actions. You will find that the people can literally feel your love even from behind a closed door or from a glance across the street. Your feelings for the people will be evident in everything you do and the more you cultivate and demonstrate that love, the less likely it is you will receive revilings.

Sometimes, rejection and difficulty are a sign that great blessing are just around the corner. Look at Alma and the sons of Mosiah on their missions. They went to serve among a people that were characterized as a wild, ferocious and a bloodthirsty people bent on destroying the Nephites at all cost. This would certainly have been the most difficult area in the mission, yet they had tremendous success. It took many years, but they literally changed an entire nation of people and so far-reaching was the effect of their missionary work that the Lamanites became more righteous than the Nephites for quite some time.

Just as Joseph Smith recorded that a thick darkness had gathered around him just before he beheld the Father and the Son, so sometimes the rejection we receive brings in dark clouds of doubt or fear just before there is a great harvest. The adversary pulls out all of the stops and tries everything to dissuade us just when the prize is within reach. This will become a frequent pattern for you and you will know that when things are getting really rough, there may be a beautiful blessing waiting for you behind the next door.

It may require a rewiring of your thinking in order to see the positive in the negative. Look at the picture on the opposite page. There are eight circles connected by lines. Now I want you to put the numbers 1 to 8 in those circles with one catch. No two consecutive numbers can be connected by any line! Go ahead and work on this for a moment, it really is possible. As a matter of fact there are several solutions. When you have either figured it out or given up, come back here. I promise I will still be here waiting no matter how long you spend on it.

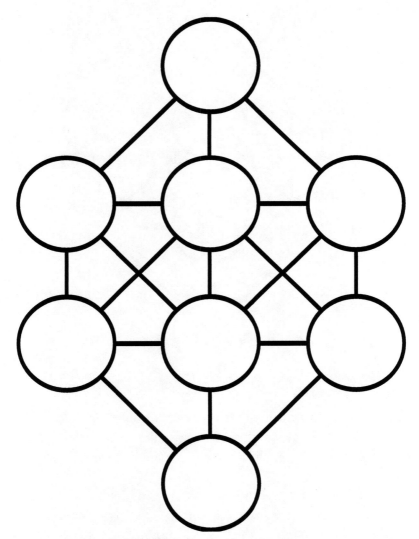

If you are really frustrated, one of the several potential answers is on the next page **BUT DON'T PEEK UNTIL YOU HAVE GIVEN IT A GOOD EFFORT!!**

The point of this exercise it that sometimes something

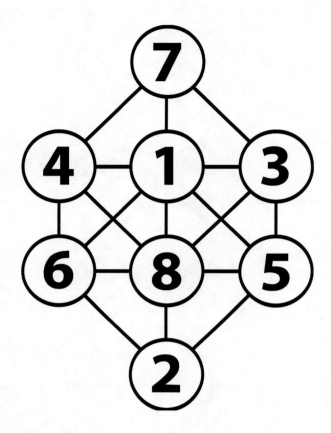

might seem very difficult or even impossible, but given time, you can do it. Dealing with adversity takes most people a long time to learn but once it has been learned, it can change your life.

Let me give you a couple of examples of dealing with adversity by looking at it from a different perspective. When I was a senior in high school, I decided I wanted to graduate halfway through my senior year so I could get some college under my belt before I went on my mission. I took the appropriate summer school classes before my senior year and made arrangements with my principal to get all of my credits by

Christmas time. The only thing I needed to do before the Christmas break was to take a paper around to my teachers and have them sign it as proof that I was passing their classes with at least a B average. I went from class to class and my teachers were happy to sign it. When I went to see my English teacher she said that I was getting an A and asked me what the letter was for. I told her that I was going to be leaving to go to college. She asked me where I was going to go and I told her Brigham Young University. Her countenance changed and she asked for the paper back. Then she pulled out her student record book and began looking at my scores again. She said things like "You know, on this test I really didn't think you answers were very complete." Then she changed the A to a C-. She looked at the next assignment and made a similar comment, once again lowering my grade. By the time she was done, she announced that my real grade would be a C. She erased the A on the form and replaced it with a C.

I was shocked! I felt like I had not only been doing well in the class but that she and I had been getting along quite well. I took the form to the principal and when he looked at it he said "Remember Lyman, we agreed that in order for this early graduation to happen you needed to be getting at least a B in all of your classes." Then he looked at the report. He said "What is this C in English?" I told him that she had changed it from an A to a C. He looked closely and said he could see the faint A under the C. Then he said "You didn't tell her where you were going did you?" I told him that I had. He said my English teacher was extremely anti-Mormon and that I should not have told her where I was going. He said he would have a talk with her and not to worry.

I don't know if he spoke to her or just changed the grade himself, but the paperwork finally did go through. On the last day of school before the break I saw my English teacher walking down the hall. I walked up to her and put my arm around her shoulder. I was a good foot taller than her and I think she thought I was going to hit her or something because she cringed a little. I looked her square in the eyes and called her by her name and said "I just wanted you to know that I really appreciate how much you have taught me this year in English. It has been a great class and I have learned a lot. I think you have helped prepare me very well for college and I wanted you to know that you are appreciated!" I let go of her and walked down the long hall to the exit doors. When I got to the doors I looked back and she was still standing right where I had left her. I think she was in shock.

On another occasion I was returning from my dad's office, having helped him do some cleaning, and I had two garbage bags in the trunk of my car. I went to the gas station that I always went to and thought that I would go around back where the dumpster was and put these two bags in it before I filled up my tank. I drove an old gas guzzler and spent many hundreds of dollars at this specific station. Seeing that it was only about 1/4 full, I put the two bags in the dumpster and was just about to get back into the car when the manager came running around the corner. He began to shout at me and told me he wasn't paying to have my garbage hauled away! He told me to get my crap out of his dumpster and get the #@*! out of there. I apologized and took my two bags back out and put them into my trunk. He kept yelling and began to pull junk out of the dumpster and throw it into my trunk. There were liquor bottles and pieces of food and all kinds of filthy garbage that wasn't part of my two trash bags. He kept throwing stuff in until he felt satisfied and then he slammed the trunk and told me to get lost.

I got into the car and drove around to the front of the station and stopped at a pump and began to pump gas. It was one of those stations where the manager sits in a booth right in between two pumps. I was at the pump closest to where he was sitting on his stool at the register. As I began to pump the gas, a worried look came across his face. I don't know if he thought I was going to steal the gas or if he thought that I was going to break something but he was definitely worried. He watched the pump as the dollars rang up higher and higher. My tank was pretty low and it was going to take quite a bit of money to fill it. In order to stop him from worrying, I got out my wallet and began to count cash so it would be obvious that I intended to pay for it. As soon as he saw the money, he came out of the booth and calmly said, "You know what? I have another dumpster on the other side of the lot and it doesn't have anything in it. Would you like to empty your trash in that one?" I paid for the gas and he helped me get the garbage emptied.

If I had left angry from either of these situations, everyone involved would have remained angry. By simply thinking of another way to respond in the situations, I think everyone left with a good feeling—a little confused maybe, but without any indignation.

The last story is one that I read in a magazine many years ago about a woman who moved into a new neighborhood. When one of the neighbors went over to welcome her they asked her how she liked the neighborhood. She replied that it was fine except for the man who ran the drug store. She said that she had been in the store and that the man had been rude and took forever to help her with what she needed. She even told the neighbor to be sure and tell the man at the store how she felt and how poor his service was.

The following week, the new lady went to her neighbor and said, "You must have really told that old coot down at the drug store what a idiot he was and what a lousy job he did when I was in there last week. I went in there today and he greeted me with a pleasant smile and immediately asked me how he could help me. He quickly got what I needed and cordially walked me to the counter and quickly rang me up. It was a great experience. You must have really told him off!" The neighbor looked at the lady and said, "I hope you will forgive me, but I didn't do quite what you asked me to do. You see, when I went in to the drug store, I told the man there that you had been in last week. He remembered you. I told him that you had told me that he was the nicest man and that he had been so helpful and kind that you would be back next week."

Learn to look for the better way to handle rejection.

Now let's talk about facing opposition from your companion. This is something that I hope you never have to deal with and I certainly hope you never instigate! There are valid reasons for opposing your companion's actions and there are ridiculous reasons. The way to distinguish is to simply ask yourself, "Does this action have eternal consequences?" If the answer is 'yes' and the consequences are negative, you must oppose your companion. If the consequences are not eternal, don't let it bother you and try to find something positive on which to focus.

Let me give you an example of both types of items. If my companion wanted to do something that required the flagrant breaking of the mission rules such as going to a movie, I would oppose that idea. Or if he were to say, "Let's not work today. Instead I think we need to refresh ourselves by going down to the beach and spending the morning." This kind of thing does have eternal consequences. On the other hand, if my companion likes to slice tomatoes thicker than I like them, who really cares? I can eat them just as easily and, who knows, maybe I'll even like them better that way. If my companion likes the toilet tissue to roll from the top and I have always liked it to roll from the bottom, who really cares? These thing are just not eternally significant.

The best way to handle the non eternal problems is with simple discussion. Remember to be flexible and to try to find a solution even if it means that you are the one doing the changing. Don't get caught up in the thick of thin things. It's not worth the waste of time.

The problems that are of an eternal nature must be handled quickly and without the slightest room for acceptance. You must not agree to go to the movies with your companion three or four times and then finally get a conscience and try to mend it. Don't do things that will jeopardize your companionship with the Holy Ghost or you will become ineffective in the work.

If your companion is the senior and suggests something that you know is not right and is of eternal significance, tell him you will not participate and if he persists, call your priesthood leader immediately whether it be a district leader, zone leader, or the mission president and let them know without delay what is going on. Make sure that your companion realizes that you are doing this because of your love for him and your love for your mission and your love for the Lord. Are you your brothers keeper? YES!

In his second epistle to the Corinthians, Paul said "Finally, brethren, farewell. Be perfect, be of good comfort, be of one mind, live in peace; and the God of love and peace shall be with you." (2 Cor. 13:11) If you and your companion have a disagreement about something, talk about it and come to a resolution. Be of "one mind" so you can do the work. One of the very first things that the Savior taught when he appeared on the American continent was that contention is of the devil. "For verily, verily I say unto you, he that hath the spirit of contention is not of me, but is of the devil, who is the father of contention, and he stirreth up the hearts of men to contend with anger, one with another (3 Nephi 11:29). If the devil is successful in causing contention between companions, he doesn't have to do anything else to stop the work from progressing because the harmony will leave the companionship and the spirit will cease to strive with that companionship.

Thus, the work of the Lord will stop.

If your companion reproves you justly, take it in humility and know that he loves you. I had a zone leader come to our area on a trade off and when we were done working he had a stewardship meeting with me. He told me that my companion and I were doing fine and everything was OK. I asked him if there was anything on which we could improve. He said no. Then I asked him if he loved me. He looked at me for a minute and then said he did. I told him that if he really loved me he would help me to be a better missionary and if he needed to reprove me, that would demonstrate that love. He paused for a moment and then told me two things that he felt I needed to improve on. He hadn't brought them up before because he was afraid of hurting my feelings. When he understood that my feelings would be hurt more if he knew ways I could improve and wouldn't tell me, he helped me to see what I could do to improve. That demonstrated to me that he really cared.

Reproving and directing in righteousness show love and compassion. Don't be afraid to show it or receive it. The Lord said . . .

"No power or influence can or ought to be maintained by virtue of the priesthood, only by persuasion, by long-suffering, by gentleness and meekness, and by love unfeigned; By kindness, and pure knowledge, which shall greatly enlarge the soul without hypocrisy, and without guile— Reproving betimes with sharpness, when moved upon by the Holy Ghost; and then showing forth afterwards an increase of love toward him whom thou hast reproved, lest he esteem thee to be his enemy; That he may know that thy faithfulness is stronger than the cords of death" (D&C 121:41-44).

Show forth that increase in love and they will hopefully understand.

If you know of missionaries who are doing things that are

wrong and that are of eternal significance, do something about it!

I had an experience with a couple of missionaries who were doing things they should not have been doing. One evening, while my companion and I were out in another zone following up on a Spanish-speaking referral, we saw two missionaries at the top of the street going into a store. (I was a Spanish-speaking missionary in Sydney Australia and we were allowed to travel anywhere in the mission to take care of Spanish referrals.) I noticed that the two missionaries we saw were not wearing their suit jackets. We had a mission rule that after 6:00 p.m. we were to wear our suit jackets. It was much later than that and so I told my companion we should go up to the store and give them a hard time about not having on their jackets. I didn't think that not having their jackets on was a major event, after all, when we did referrals that took us a lot longer to travel to than we expected, we sometimes were left without our coats after 6:00 p.m. I just thought we'd have some fun with them and tease them about it. When we entered the store and walked up to them, they literally turned white when they saw us.

I went up to one of them and said something about their lack of coats. I smiled and laughed and he looked at me, reached up and put his hand on my shoulder (I am almost a foot taller than he) and he said "I'm glad it was you who found us, someone else would have turned us in." I thought to myself, you really think someone would turn you in for being caught without your coats?

Having made their purchases, we began to walk out of the store. It was very obvious that these two Elders were trying to separate my companion and I so they could talk to us. We had been walking toward the train station for a few minutes when it occurred to me that these two Elders were not companions! As a matter of fact, they were not even in the same district!!

They weren't even in the same zone!!! I remembered that they both had been given new Elders to train on the same day that I had been given my current companion to train. I asked the Elder who was walking by me where his companion was. He looked at me as though he had been found out and then he got this grin on his face and told me that both of their companions, thinking they were involved in a legitimate trade off, had been sent as a companionship to the red light district as a joke!

These new Elders were so new that they would not have known how to get back to their apartments very easily and there could have been some real trouble. I asked him how they were going to get home and he laughed and said they'd find the way. I was in shock! I couldn't believe my ears! What I did not realize is that this was just the tip of the iceberg. Before he told me anything else, he again put his hand on my shoulder and told me that he was glad I had found them because someone else would have turned them in. Then he invited my companion and I to a birthday party for an elder in his district (both of these elders were serving as district leaders in different zones). He told me it would be held in a sauna room downtown on a Wednesday morning. I was appalled. Not only was downtown off limits and not only was Wednesday not a preparation day, but the place they were going to was definitely not appropriate for missionaries.

I continued to listen to what he was saying and let him tell me more and more about the things that these two districts were doing and the amazing amount of rules that were being broken.

One of the things that disturbed me the most was the consistent lying on the reports that they were turning in to the zone leaders. They lied about time spent working and the number of discussions being taught, etc. He told me all of these things in the thirty-minute walk to the train station. We were both taking the same train back toward our areas. Just before we got on the train, once again he put his hand on my shoulder and said how glad he was that I had found them because, you guessed it, someone else would have turned them in.

As we sat on the train, I asked my companion what he and the other Elder had talked about and he said they had talked about where he was from, etc. Just your general small talk. The other Elders sat in a different car of the train and got off a few stops before ours. When we reached our stop, I told my companion that we were not going to exit the train but that we had to stay on and go to see our zone leaders. We stayed on the train until it came to the town where the zone leaders lived and walked to their apartment. It was after 11:00 p.m. when we arrived. I knocked on the door until one of the Elders came and opened it. He looked at me, shook his head, and looked again. He asked what I needed and I told him I needed to talk to him alone in the hall for a moment. My companion went into the room and I spent the next several minutes telling this Elder what I had been told. My main concern at that point was to help those brand new Elders find their way home.

When I was finished, the zone leader went right to the phone and called the mission home. The Mission President and his assistants got in the car and began looking for the new Elders. They found them talking to a prostitute on a street corner and trying to place a copy of the Book Of Mormon with her. The Mission President took them home and raised the roof with the two districts. All of the missionaries were split up and the two leaders were sent to almost opposite ends of the mission. I was asked to go with the zone leader to effectuate the transfers.

One of the Elders was very humble and repentant. When we entered his apartment we found him packing, in tears and apologizing for what had happened. The other Elder (this was the one who kept putting his hand on my shoulder) was quite different, even belligerent. He asked me in a sarcastic voice if I had been made a zone leader for turning them in. He said I must feel pretty good getting to be a zone leader now and being able to gloat over their terrible situation.

I tried to tell him how much I loved him and how much I loved the work and the Lord. I told him I hoped that one day he would see that I turned them in for that love and not for any other reason. He could not understand that love could be the motivation for getting him into so much trouble. He could not see that his new companion could have been in serious trouble. Nor could he see that by leading the entire district into disobedient behavior, he was soiling the reputation of the church and not only halting the current work but damaging the work for years to come.

Don't ever let this type of opposition get in the way of the work of the Lord. There is no question that this carried potential eternal consequences. The time to act when you find this type of disobedience is **NOW**! Imagine how much better it would have been if any one of the Elders in either of the districts had simply said "**No, I will not participate in that!**" It would not have progressed very far. Imagine if they had continued and one of the Elders had called the zone leader or the Mission President. This problem could have been caught at the beginning and the harm caused could have been minimal. Make sure you are **NEVER** part of the problem!!

Now I will relate another story of opposition from a companion. One morning the zone leaders showed up and told my companion and me we were going to have transfers. My new companion would be an Elder that I already knew from the LTM (the old term for the MTC). While in the LTM we had some difficult times and did not fit well together. Now the prospect of having that companionship renewed was disheartening. I knew this Elder did not like me. He had expressed that very clearly in the LTM. I held out small hope that his feelings might have changed in the previous three or four months.

It became evident that they had not. After we had been together a short time, he contracted a cold and, as the senior companion, he said we would not go out tracting that day. I told him I was glad not to be sick and I would mark some Book of Mormons for distribution (we used to mark specific passages in the books for the people to read). I went down the hall to take a shower (there was only one shower for all sixteen apartments) and when I came back into the room, there my companion was violently coughing into my pillow. He had taken it off my bed and was using it to cough into.

On another occasion when we were shopping for our weekly groceries, I noticed that he has spent about 1/4 the amount that I had spent. I asked him what he was going to eat during the week and he told me not to worry. I had purchased some bologna with seven slices in a resealable pack. I would use one slice on a sandwich each day for the week. On the second day, I got out the bologna and pulled off a piece to put on my bread and noticed that all of the remaining slices had had the middle cut out of them to within a half of an inch of the outside edge. My companion was enjoying a rather thick bologna sandwich!

One of our mission rules was to keep our shoes polished. We were asked to polish them every day. One morning, having polished my shoes, I went down to the shower. When I returned I found my companion with his hands in my shoes scuffing them together to ruin the shine. I asked him what he was doing and he suggested that he was simply seeing how durable the shine on the shoes was and how much punishment it could take.

One morning I noticed that my orange juice was very bland. It tasted like orange water. I thought that was strange because the day before it had tasted fine. (I used to buy 2 liter bottles of orange juice.) Then one day, when I came up from the shower, I found my companion with a huge glass of orange juice on the counter. He was at the sink filling my jug back up with water to the level it had been before he had taken the huge drink. No wonder it had tasted weak, it was full of water!

On another occasion as I began to pour my cereal into my bowl in the morning, the bag fell out of the box and onto the table, followed by a bunch of trash. I was confused until I realized that my companion had been eating my cereal and didn't want me to see the level of cereal going down so he would roll up the bottom of the cereal bag and put trash in the bottom of the box. I guess he hoped we would be transferred before the bag fell out!

There are many more instances that I could relate to you here but these few will suffice. How do these things make you feel? There are many possible emotions all the way from rage to pity. The important question is the one posed above. Are these things eternal in their consequences? I guess you could argue to some extent for both 'yes' and 'no,' but I determined in my mind that they were not eternal in nature and just chose to ignore them. I stood 6'4" and at that time weighed roughly 250 pounds, so there were many options available to try to resolve the problem, but ignoring it seemed to be the best and I was able to keep the Spirit with me.

You might ask if I tried to talk to my companion about these things and the many others not mentioned. I tried at first, but it became highly evident that that avenue was not going to change anything. So I determined that it was not eternal and thus I would be better off simply forgetting about it.

Some of you may end up having similar experiences and some will not, but the important thing is to make sure that you are not giving that experience to another missionary.

Now for a little experiment. I want you to look at the next page and tell me what you see.

Now that you have looked at the page, what did you see? Did you see a blob or mark on the page? Maybe you thought it looked like something. Or did you see a beautiful white sheet of paper with unlimited potential for words or pictures or anything else, perhaps even origami? I hope you focused on the positive and not the little blemish.

You will find opposition in the mission field. If you didn't, you would not be doing the Lord's work because there is opposition in all things. "For it must needs be, that there is an opposition in all things. If not so, my first-born in the wilderness, righteousness could not be brought to pass, neither wickedness, neither holiness nor misery, neither good nor bad (2 Ne. 2: 11).

I hope that you will focus on the positive and learn to overlook the negatives in you life. They negatives are small when compared to the eternal things.

Even if it seems like negative is all around you and there is no way out, concentrate on the positive no matter how small and you will actually feel the negative fading away. Look at the picture on the next page and focus on the white dot in the middle for ten or fifteen seconds. As you continue to focus, the gray outer area begins to vanish. So it is with the negatives that seem at times to surround us. Focus on the positive and they will seem to disappear.

Now for your assignment. Think of anything that you perceive as negative or hurting and weigh it against the things of eternity. See how significant they really are. Secondly I want you to look for the positive in everything you do for the next week and try not to focus on the negative. As Mary Poppins so well stated "In every job that must be done there is an element of fun, you find the fun and snap! The job's a game." Be positive and notice how those around you become more positive as well. If you find yourself being negative, stop and immediately think about something positive. If you keep it up, it will eventually become a habit to look for the good in any situation. That will help you in many aspects of life.

What do you see in the picture below? Turn the book upside down and see what you find. Be willing to turn things around and find the good in any given situation.

# CHAPTER 2

# SLOWING DOWN THE FAST

Fasting is potentially one of the best known and yet one of the least kept principles of the gospel. Think for a moment, how does your family go about fasting? How do you personally participate in fasting? Are the two different? Does your "fast" seem "slow?" Are you glad when you are put on the early meeting schedule for your building because you can get home and eat earlier on fast Sunday? Is fast Sunday something you look forward to or something you dread? Do you find occasionally that just when you are putting cereal in a bowl, Mom or Dad comes in and reminds you it's fast Sunday and you are extremely disappointed?

Let's take a moment and determine how to turn your fast into a source of POWER rather than a source of hunger.

Get out a piece of paper and write down as many reasons for fasting as you can. Now I really want you to do this–get out a piece of paper and make the list. I'll wait, I'm not going anywhere so really get out the paper. Stop reading until you have at least five reasons listed for fasting.

Let's explore just some of the things that might be on your list:

Supply money for those in need.
Receive financial blessings.
Gain humility
It's a commandment.
Gain spiritual power.
Purify the soul.

Cleanse the body.
Heal the sick.
Baptize.

Now that you have a list, let's consider how fasting affects some of the items on the list. My list is certainly not exhaustive so if your list contains different items, that's great; take the time to ponder how fasting will affect those particular items.

First, let's look at fasting as a means of supplying money for the needs of the less fortunate. When we fast, we are asked to fast through two meals and then donate the money saved from those two meals to the bishop for distribution to the needy. Of course this principle is not necessarily one of the letter of the law. You don't need to add up the cost of each egg, each slice of bread, each teaspoon of butter, each cup of milk and the gas to go to the store to get them, etc., in order to determine how much to give the bishop. The brethren have simply asked us to give generously. President Spencer W. Kimball said: "Sometimes we have been a bit penurious [unwilling to share] and figured that we had for breakfast one egg and that cost so many cents and then we give that to the Lord. I think that when we are affluent, as many of us are, that we ought to be very, very generous . . . and give, instead of the amount we saved by our two meals of fasting, perhaps much, much more—ten times more where we are in a position to do it" (in Conference Report, Apr. 1974, 184).

Matthew Cowley said on one occasion when speaking to some of the saints in the Islands that he was thinking of moving his family to live among them because according to the fast offering receipts, it would only cost .03¢ a meal to live! (see Matthew Cowley, Ask and It Shall Be Given You, Covenant Recordings, Inc. 1979).

As the Church grows we find ourselves with more opportunities to help through donations to the fast offering funds.

These funds are turned in to the Church and distributed where needed. This great law is the Lord's way to supply for the needs of all of his people. Along with tithing and the other donations we make, fast offerings prepare us to eventually live the law of consecration in its fullness.

Next, let's look at the potential financial blessings for obeying the law of the fast. President Spencer W. Kimball stated, "If we give a generous fast offering, we shall increase our own prosperity both spiritually and temporally" (Ensign, Nov. 1977, p. 79). Marion G. Romney said, "If we will double our fast offerings, we shall increase our own prosperity, both spiritually and temporally. This the Lord has promised, and this has been the record" (address to the Priesthood Board, Mar. 6, 1974, p. 10). Through payment of tithing we are promised the windows of heaven will be open and will bestow blessings to the extent that we will not have enough room to receive them all. These blessings are not necessarily financial. The Lord's law of finance is really the law of the fast.

Fasting is a great way to remind ourselves that we are totally dependent on the Lord for virtually everything. Without Him we could not even draw another breath. Fasting reminds us that the food we eat and the liquids we drink are all provided to us by the Lord. What a lesson in humility! Obedience to this law will bring us closer to Him upon whom we are totally reliant. We can approach Him in sincere prayer during a fast in a way which may not be possible by any other method.

Of course, fasting is a commandment. "Also, I give unto you a commandment that ye shall continue in prayer and fasting from this time forth" (D&C 88:76). The reason we are commanded to fast is the same reason that we have any of the commandments: to bless our lives! We can gain so much from fasting that will bring us closer to God that He has made it a commandment to do it.

We can gain great spiritual power by observing the law of

the fast. "Nevertheless they did fast and pray oft, and did wax stronger and stronger in their humility, and firmer and firmer in the faith of Christ, unto the filling their souls with joy and consolation, yea, even to the purifying and the sanctification of their hearts, which sanctification cometh because of their yielding their hearts unto God" (Helaman 3:35). As you can see, fasting can lead to purifying ourselves and sanctifying our hearts by giving them to God.

Fasting is good for the body. It cleanses your body physically and helps you to feel what those who are in need feel. It can also help when there is a situation that requires fasting because of lack of food or drink. A man spoke in a meeting that I attended several years ago and told the story of him and his wife going to the Soviet Union on a tour of some kind. While on the tour, it was discovered that some of the food they had was rancid and was causing some of the tourists to become ill. They were told that the food could not be replaced for twenty-four hours. This man and his wife who were used to fasting we able to deal with the twenty-four-hour fast much better than the other tourists who became so ill that several had to be transported to hospitals. Some were so ill that they could not eat the new food when it arrived. This man told us how grateful he was that he and his wife were used to fasting and were able to endure the experience with hardly any ill effects at all.

We can fast for those who are ill. David fasted for his son who was gravely ill. "And when they were come to the multitude, there came to him a certain man, kneeling down to him, and saying, Lord, have mercy on my son: for he is lunatick, and sore vexed: for ofttimes he falleth into the fire, and oft into the water. And I brought him to thy disciples, and they could not cure him. Then Jesus answered and said, O faithless and perverse generation, how long shall I be with you? how long shall I suffer you? bring him hither to me. And Jesus rebuked the devil; and he departed out of him: and the child was cured from that very hour. Then came the disciples to Jesus apart, and said, Why could not we cast him out? And Jesus said unto them, Because of your unbelief: for verily I say unto you, If ye have faith as a grain of mustard seed, ye shall say unto this mountain, Remove hence to yonder place; and it shall remove; and nothing shall be impossible unto you. Howbeit this kind goeth not out but by prayer and fasting" (Matt 17:14-21). Many miracles come from fasting and prayer.

I hope you have read the incredible story of Alma the younger and the sons of Mosiah. These were wicked men who sought to destroy the Church in any way they could. They were idolatrous and spoke flattering words among the people but were converted to the gospel in a miraculous manner. Although I mentioned them in the first chapter to discuss the opposition they faced, I want to discuss here what brought about their success.

"Now the sons of Mosiah were numbered among the unbelievers; and also one of the sons of Alma was numbered among them, he being called Alma, after his father; nevertheless, he became a very wicked and an idolatrous man. And he was a man of many words, and did speak much flattery to the people; therefore he led many of the people to do after the manner of his iniquities. And he became a great hinderment to the prosperity of the church of God; stealing away the hearts of the people; causing much dissension among the people; giving a chance for the enemy of God to exercise his power over them. And now it came to pass that while he was going about to destroy the church of God, for he did go about secretly with the sons of Mosiah seeking to destroy the church, and to lead astray the people of the Lord, contrary to the commandments of God, or even the king—

And as I said unto you, as they were going about rebelling

against God, behold, the angel of the Lord appeared unto them; and he descended as it were in a cloud; and he spake as it were with a voice of thunder, which caused the earth to shake upon which they stood; And so great was their astonishment, that they fell to the earth, and understood not the words which he spake unto them. Nevertheless he cried again, saying: Alma, arise and stand forth, for why persecutest thou the church of God? For the Lord hath said: This is my church, and I will establish it; and nothing shall overthrow it, save it is the transgression of my people. And again, the angel said: Behold, the Lord hath heard the prayers of his people, and also the prayers of his servant, Alma, who is thy father; for he has prayed with much faith concerning thee that thou mightest be brought to the knowledge of the truth; therefore, for this purpose have I come to convince thee of the power and authority of God, that the prayers of his servants might be answered according to their faith. And now behold, can ye dispute the power of God? For behold, doth not my voice shake the earth? And can ye not also behold me before you? And I am sent from God. Now I say unto thee: Go, and remember the captivity of thy fathers in the land of Helam, and in the land of Nephi; and remember how great things he has done for them; for they were in bondage, and he has delivered them. And now I say unto thee, Alma, go thy way, and seek to destroy the church no more, that their prayers may be answered, and this even if thou wilt of thyself be cast off. And now it came to pass that these were the last words which the angel spake unto Alma, and he departed. And now Alma and those that were with him fell again to the earth, for great was their astonishment; for with their own eyes they had beheld an angel of the Lord; and his voice was as thunder, which shook the earth; and they knew that there was nothing save the power of God that could shake the earth and cause it to tremble as though it would part asunder. And now the astonishment of Alma was so great that he became dumb, that he could not open his mouth; yea, and he became weak, even that he could not move his hands; therefore he was taken by those that were with him, and carried helpless, even until he was laid before his father. And they rehearsed unto his father all that had happened unto them; and his father rejoiced, for he knew that it was the power of God. And he caused that a multitude should be gathered together that they might witness what the Lord had done for his son, and also for those that were with him. And he caused that the priests should assemble themselves together; and they began to *fast*, and to pray to the Lord their God that he would open the mouth of Alma, that he might speak, and also that his limbs might receive their strength—that the eyes of the people might be opened to see and know of the goodness and glory of God. And it came to pass after they had fasted and prayed for the space of two days and two nights, the limbs of Alma received their strength, and he stood up and began to speak unto them, bidding them to be of good comfort: For, said he, I have repented of my sins, and have been redeemed of the Lord; behold I am born of the Spirit. And the Lord said unto me: Marvel not that all mankind, yea, men and women, all nations, kindreds, tongues and people, must be born again; yea, born of God, changed from their carnal and fallen state, to a state of righteousness, being redeemed of God, becoming his sons and daughters; And thus they become new creatures; and unless they do this, they can in nowise inherit the kingdom of God (Mosiah 27:8-26, italics added).

After their dramatic conversion to the gospel, these brethren first decided to go out and preach the gospel to those who they had driven from the truth. They sought to repair the wrong they had done. Then they determined to go into the mission field away from their home much like you but with one great exception, they went out among a ferocious and blood-thirsty people (see Mosiah 10:12). Think of a people on the earth who would hate you more than anything else and who would be very anxious to kill you if they saw you. That is the area to which these faithful missionaries set out to preach the word of the Lord. Each of the sons of Mosiah were given the chance to be the king of the land but turned it down to serve their missions.

Were they successful? Of course they were, or I wouldn't have bothered to put this story in this book! The heading for Alma chapter four says that Alma baptized thousands, and that's before he gets his mission companion, Amulek! When he and Amulek go out to do the work, we not only receive great doctrine from their experiences contending with Zeezrom, but they are successful in establishing the church throughout the land!

What about the sons of Mosiah? Were they successful? Once again, would I bring it up if they were not? Of course not. I will not reprint Alma chapters 17 - 26 here but I will ask you to stop here and read them. It won't take very long and you will get a great feel for the success that they had. Stop now and read. I mean it. I will be here when you get back.

DID YOU READ IT? I CERTAINLY HOPE SO. THAT WAY IT IS FRESH IN YOUR MIND.

As missionaries, you should fast to bring the gospel to those who do not have it. "Nevertheless the children of God were commanded that they should gather themselves together oft, and join in *fasting and mighty prayer* in behalf of the welfare of the souls of those who knew not God" (Alma 6:6). "But this is not all; they had given themselves to *much prayer, and fasting*; therefore they had the spirit of prophecy, and the spirit of revelation, and when they taught, they *taught with power* and authority of God" (Alma 17:3).

"And it came to pass that they journeyed many days in the wilderness, and they *fasted much and prayed much* that the Lord would grant unto them a portion of his Spirit to go with them, and abide with them, that they might be an instrument in the hands of God to bring, if it were possible, their brethren, the Lamanites, to the knowledge of the truth, to the knowledge of the baseness of the traditions of their fathers, which were not correct" (Alma 17:9) (all italics added).

These righteous men fasted and prayed so that they would have power when they taught so that they could bring the knowledge of the truth to these hardened people. They served separately for fourteen years and all remained faithful. They baptized thousands and thousands who were so converted to the gospel that they virtually stopped fighting against their bitter enemies.

You can have the power of fasting in your work. It can help you to teach with the power of God unto the changing of hearts. How can you get that power? Follow the law of the fast.

Now let's discuss the ingredients of a proper fast. First let's consider the length of time for a proper fast. As we mentioned above, the Lord has requested that "One Sunday each month Latter-day Saints observe a fast day. On this day we neither eat nor drink for two consecutive meals, thus making a fast of twenty-four hours. If we were to eat our evening meal on Saturday, then we would not eat or drink until the evening meal on Sunday" (31110, Gospel Principles, Unit Seven: Perfecting Our Lives, 25: Fasting, 165).

On this point there is some misunderstanding. There are some that think that the fast is over when they get home from church no matter the time. They feel that they are lucky when they are on the early block so they can get home and eat earlier. The true fast consists of twenty-four hours, as mentioned above. If you eat a late dinner on Saturday night, you should fast through breakfast and lunch the following day and not eat until late on Sunday night. If you would like to have your fast end Sunday at noon, you should not eat dinner on Saturday nor breakfast on Sunday morning. As you can see, the meeting block time should not be an issue.

The next ingredient for a proper fast is to begin with a prayer. This can be personal or family prayer but it should accompany fasting. Fasting without prayer is hunger. Prayer demonstrates the purpose for your fast. Talk with God about your reason for fasting. Express to him what you are trying to accomplish. Ask for His help in gaining the humility of the fast and ask Him to help you to "feel" the fast spiritually. Don't just start fasting without expressing to God a specific purpose for the fast.

The next ingredient is focus. You must focus on your reason(s) for fasting. Keep you mind occupied with thoughts of your purpose. As the fast progresses you will find it easier to remember your purposes.

As you focus, continue to pray throughout the day for the things you are trying to accomplish. Talk to God several times about what you are doing.

Of course, proper motives are essential. If you are fasting for the wrong reasons you might as well not do it at all. Any of the things mentioned in the list would be a good reason to fast. Fasting for a new boat might not be in harmony with the law of the fast whereas fasting for a new job could very well be. Let the Holy Spirit be your guide and you will be able to accomplish your purposes.

Finally, if at all possible, end your fast with a prayer. Talk with Father again about your reasons for fasting. Express to him your gratitude for the law of the fast. You will find that if you have fasted properly you will not have feelings of hunger for food and drink but for the Spirit. Many times at the conclusion of a fast I have been surrounded by food and it has had no effect on me and I do not feel the need to partake until I have ended my fast with a heartfelt prayer.

How often you should fast is something you should discuss with the Lord. Of course you should partake of the regular fast day with the Church but beyond that you must be prudent and wise knowing that to much fasting can cause health problems. The Priesthood Bulletin stated in June 1972, "We are informed that some missionaries engage in rather lengthy fasting. It is not advisable that they do this. If there is a special matter for which they should fast, then they would fast one day and then go to the Lord humbly and ask for His blessing. That should suffice. If our missionaries feel the need of fasting, they should fast for the day only and not extend it. They need the strength for their work, and I think once a month is sufficient for fasting. They may have special occasions when they want to increase their faith to help someone who is ill or for other worthy causes when they may take another day during the month, but they should not make a prolonged fast" (Priesthood Bulletin, Vol.8, no. 3 [June 1972], pp. 5-6).

Fasting properly will give you power and humility. It will bring you closer to God and help you to understand who you are in His kingdom. It can bring to pass much righteousness. If you look at it as a burden instead of an opportunity you will simply feel hunger and thirst and will be anxious for it to end. If you let it work for you, you will feel the blessings of heaven pouring upon you.

One last comment: I have heard it said that prayer is like shining a flashlight toward heaven. The light certainly ascends and reaches heaven, but if you add fasting to your prayers, it is like turning the flashlight into a high power spotlight and shining it toward heaven. It just seems a little easier to reach the throne of God with more intensity in our prayers when they are coupled with fasting.

Now for your assignment. It is fairly easy. Next Saturday and Sunday, fast properly. Start Saturday at noon if possible and conclude Sunday at noon. Do it with a purpose and follow all of the steps to make the fast a wonderful experience. I promise you that you will begin to look forward to the opportunity of fasting and prayer. That is why the scriptures refer to it as rejoicing and prayer and fullness of joy (See D&C 59:13-14).

# CHAPTER 3

# PRAYER: IN THE PRESENCE OF GOD

It is impossible to talk about fasting without discussing prayer. As James Montgomery put it when he penned one of the most heartfelt of the hymns, prayer is the soul's sincere desire, uttered or unexpressed. It is through prayer that we approach the throne of the Father and express our deepest feelings and thoughts.

In the preexistence, our Heavenly Father was with us and we were able to converse with one another. If we had questions, we asked and He was there to answer us. If we had praise to give, we offered it and He was there to listen. If we had problems, He was there to hear them and help us. I am certain that we enjoyed our interactions with Him.

In His great wisdom, Father knew that we would need His counsel and advice, help and direction, love and expression here on earth perhaps even more than we did while in His presence. For that reason and because He loves us so much and wanted to communicate with us while we were here, He ordained the principle of prayer. What a marvelous blessing to be able to communicate in the most intimate way with our loving Father who yearns to give us the counsel and help that we so desperately need!

I was an adult before I understood that there is specific reason that we pray in the sacred name of Jesus Christ. I had assumed that it was because Christ was Father's right hand man as far as the earth goes and it showed respect to include

Christ in our prayers. But it goes so much further than that. In the Book of Timothy we read, "For there is one God, and one mediator between God and men, the man Christ Jesus" (1 Tim 2:5). In the writings of John the Savior said, "I am the way, the truth, and the life: no man cometh unto the Father, but by me" (John 14:6). I believe that Christ carries our prayers to the Father and carries the answers to our prayers from the Father to us.

Though we pray properly to the Father, our prayers are imperfect and lacking. Only things of perfection can be before our Father. The Savior taught the Nephites that "no unclean thing can enter into his kingdom; therefore nothing entereth into his rest save it be those who have washed their garments in my blood, because of their faith, and the repentance of all their sins, and their faithfulness unto the end" (3 Nephi 27:19). If our prayers are not perfect enough to go directly to the Father, we need someone who can "purify" them for us. Some one who knows us well enough to know exactly what the real intent of our prayers are and who can bring them to the throne of the Father for us. Of course, that Being is the Mediator for us all, even Jesus Christ.

"When we use these sacred words, 'in the name of Jesus Christ,' they are much more than a way to get out of a prayer, a testimony, or a talk. We are on holy ground, brothers and sisters. We are using a name most sublime, most holy, and most wonderful—the very name of the Son of God. We are now able to come unto the Father through His Beloved Son. What power and reassurance and peace come when we really pray in His name. This conclusion to the prayer may, in many ways, be the most important part of the prayer. We can appeal to the Father through His victorious Son with confidence that our prayers will be heard. We can ask and receive, we can seek and find and subsequently find the open door" (L. Edward Brown,

"Pray unto the Father in My Name," Ensign, May 1997, 78) (italics added).

The answers to our prayers come in the same manner. Elder Bruce R. McConkie said . . .

"It is true that when we pray to the Father, the answer comes from the Son, because 'there is . . . one mediator between God and men, the man Christ Jesus' (1 Tim. 2:5). Joseph Smith, for instance, asked the Father, in the name of the Son, for answers to questions, and the answering voice was not that of the Father but of the Son, because Christ is our advocate, our intercessor, the God (under the Father) who rules and regulates this earth.

And it is true that sometimes in his answers, Christ assumes the prerogative of speaking by divine investiture of authority as though he were the Father; that is, he speaks in the first person and uses the name of the Father because the Father has placed his own name on the Son" (Bruce R. McConkie, "Why the Lord Ordained Prayer," Ensign, Jan. 1976, 7).

Really think about it the next time you pray.

**Heavenly Father**

**Answers come through Jesus Christ from the Father**  **Jesus Christ**  **Prayers go through Jesus Christ to the Father**

**God's Children**

It is not just something that we do lightly when we pray in the name of Jesus Christ. It is not really optional. It is the only way that we can elevate the prayer into the realm of God the Father and the only way that we can receive answers.

This is a very unique thing to us as members of the Church. There are so many of our brothers and sisters throughout the world who have been taught to pray to statues or to saints. There are those among us who don't realize Christ's part in our prayers and simply end with an "amen." What a wonderful thing to know why we include Christ and how much we depend on Him! Let us always pray in the hallowed name of Jesus Christ and keep in our minds and hearts what His role is in our prayers.

Let's go over the basic steps of prayer that you will teach in the mission field and which you have probably been taught several times. First we open by addressing our Heavenly Father. Second, we thank Him for all of the blessings we have. The third step is to ask Him for the things we need and the fourth step is to close in the name of Jesus Christ. It is a simple yet wonderful and powerful process.

Elder McConkie speaks of three reasons why we pray. First, it is a commandment. One of the commandments given to our first parents was, "Wherefore, thou shalt do all that thou doest in the name of the Son, and thou shalt repent and call upon God in the name of the Son forevermore" (Moses 5:8). Later, through the prophet Joseph Smith the Lord said, "Ask, and ye shall receive; knock, and it shall be opened unto you (D&C 4:7). It is not up to us to decide whether or not we should pray. God has commanded us to pray and even said that if we don't pray, we will be had in remembrance before the judge of His people. (See D&C 68:33).

The second reason to pray is that temporal and spiritual blessings follow proper prayer. Think of the great spiritual blessing that came into the life of Alma the Younger because of the prayers of his father. "And again, the angel said: Behold, the Lord hath heard the prayers of his people, and also the prayers of his servant, Alma, who is thy father; for he has prayed with much faith concerning thee that thou mightest be brought to the knowledge of the truth; therefore, for this purpose have I come to convince thee of the power and authority of God, that the prayers of his servants might be answered according to their faith" (Mosiah 27:14). Part of receiving answers is exercising our faith. Remember when Nephi's bow broke and there was no food for the families? Nephi knew that his father could ask God where to go to look for food and that if he prayed in faith, the Lord would answer and provide for their temporal needs.

"And it came to pass that I, Nephi, did make out of wood a bow, and out of a straight stick, an arrow; wherefore, I did arm myself with a bow and an arrow, with a sling and with stones. And I said unto my father: Whither shall I go to obtain food? And it came to pass that he did inquire of the Lord, for they had humbled themselves because of my words . . . And it came to pass that the voice of the Lord said unto him: Look upon the ball, and behold the things which are written . . . And it came to pass that I, Nephi, beheld the pointers which were in the ball, that they did work according to the faith and diligence and heed which we did give unto them. And there was also written upon them a new writing, which was plain to be read, which did give us understanding concerning the ways of the Lord; and it was written and changed from time to time . . . And it came to pass that I, Nephi, did go forth up into the top of the mountain, according to the directions which were given upon the ball. And it came to pass that I did slay wild beasts, insomuch that I did obtain food for our families. And it came to pass that I did return to our tents, bearing the beasts which I had slain; and now when they beheld that I had obtained food, how great was their joy! And it came to pass that they did humble themselves before the Lord, and did give thanks unto him" (1 Nephi 16:23-32).

Notice that they gave thanks to God for the blessing they received. Our Heavenly Father desires that we express gratitude for all things that we have received at His hand. "And in nothing doth man offend God, or against none is his wrath kindled, save those who confess not his hand in all things" (D&C 59:21).

The third reason for prayer is that it is essential for our salvation. How can we think that we will be comfortable in God's kingdom if we don't know how to communicate with Him? It would be like going to a foreign country when you do not know the language; you would feel uneasy there. We must grow as close to Father as we can so we will feel truly at peace in His presence.

King Benjamin in the Book of Mormon asked the question, "For how knoweth a man the master whom he has not served, and who is a stranger unto him, and is far from the thoughts and intents of his heart?" (Mosiah 5:13). We must use every opportunity to draw closer to Him and keep our relationship fresh. "Draw near unto me and I will draw near unto you; seek me diligently and ye shall find me; ask, and ye shall receive; knock, and it shall be opened unto you" (D&C 88:63).

How long are your prayers? I really want you to think about your personal prayers. How long are they on average? One minute? Two minutes? Five minutes? Ten minutes? Thirty minutes? An hour? How long was you last prayer? When was your last prayer? I hope it was at least this morning if not during the day today. How many minutes are in a day? Let's figure it out. There are 60 minutes in each hour and 24 hours in a day, so there are 60 x 24 = 1,440 minutes in a day. How many of those minutes did you spend in prayer? What percentage? If you prayed twice a day for five minutes each time, you spent less than one percent of your time talking to God. How long did you spend talking to people who can do very little to help you back into the presence of God? How much time did you spend with a good friend talking about your problems and getting their advice?

Now let's ask this question: How long did you spend listening to God's response to your petition? Did you take the time to listen for His response? Did you ask Him for something or even a specific question and if you did, did you give Him a moment to make His answer known?

Frequently we find ourselves in the situation where we are just getting into bed and we remember that we need to pray. Sometimes we get out of bed and kneel and sometimes we lay there or sit up and offer a quick prayer. We say the same things that we have said hundreds of times and when we utter 'amen' we plop back in bed and go to sleep. Has this ever happened to you? Really think about it. If not, you are the exception to the rule.

There are so many things that we can incorporate into our prayers that it would be hard to keep a prayer under 30 minutes if we used even some of them. Amulek suggested that we pray for our crops, herds, fields, flocks, mercy and salvation (See Alma 34:17-29). James suggested that we ask for wisdom (James 1:5). Nephi suggests that we pray about everything so that our performance will be consecrated by God (2 Nephi 32:9). The Lord said that we should ask for revelation upon revelation, knowledge upon knowledge, to know the mysteries and the peaceable things (D&C 42:61). We should pray for others, for the sick and infirm, for the work to progress, for hearts to open, for the safety of others. We should pray for the leaders of the church, for the missionaries, for our families and for investigators. We should confess our sins, talk with Him about personal problems, praise Him and worship Him. We should give thanks for all our blessings.

Think of how your life would be different if you had no senses. What if you couldn't smell, touch, taste, see or hear? Are you thankful for your abilities? You have many talents that are gifts from God. Take the time to thank Him for them. Can you see where you might spend more time on your knees just in giving thanks?

Take time to think about your day before you go to bed. Think about what went well and what did not. Think about the sins you may have committed. Ponder the things that blessed your day. After taking that inventory, offer a prayer to Father and discuss it with Him. Do the same thing in the morning. When you arise, take time to think about what you are going to do for the day and talk it over with God. Ask for His help in what you want to accomplish and offer your services where He may need you. Throughout the day, carry a prayer in your heart and discuss things with Him as the day goes on. Make Him one of the friends from whom you seek advice and listen to Him like you would listen to a close friend.

Have you ever talked to someone who is so full of themselves that all they talk about is what they do or what they have accomplished? They are constantly trying to top the last story with one of their own that they feel is better or funnier or more tragic, etc. They never seem to be quiet and they talk almost exclusively about themselves. If you have never talked to someone like this, you will. It is not a very pleasant experience, yet that is kind of how we treat God when we pray and don't give Him time to respond. We talk all about our needs and wants and our blessings and our goals, etc. How hard that must be for Him to listen to us without an opportunity to respond.

Have you ever been called on the phone by someone trying to sell you something and they don't let you get a word in edgewise and if you do force a word here and there (like, no thank you) they seem to not have heard what you said and they just go on and on and on and no matter what you try to say they cut you off and continue to try to sell you the product that you don't want to buy and no matter what you do it is hopeless and you know they are going to keep you on the phone forever and you will probably be listening to them endlessly and it seems to never end and you dinner is getting cold and they don't seem to care and again you say "no thank you" and again they don't bother to listen they just keep going and going like this sentence?!!!!!        Whew! Think how frustrating it must be to Father to have one of His children, whom He loves so deeply, ask Him a question or just start a conversation where they do all of the talking and then immediately hang up! How disrespectful is that!?!

I really feel that there should be five parts to prayer and that the fifth one should be to listen. The Lord said that He stands at the door and knocks and all we have to do is let Him in. We must do this in our prayers and the way to let Him in is to listen.

THE STEPS OF PRAYER
    1. ADDRESS HEAVENLY FATHER
    2. THANK HIM FOR YOUR BLESSINGS
    3. ASK HIM FOR WHAT YOU NEED
    4. CLOSE IN THE NAME OF JESUS CHRIST
    5. LISTEN TO HIS RESPONSES

My companion and I had occasion to follow up on a Spanish-speaking referral from some missionaries that were on the other side of the mission. In order for us to get to the investigators home, we had to walk to the bus station, take the bus to the train station, take the train to the ferry, take the ferry to the other side of the harbor, catch a train to another bus station, take the bus for several miles and then we had to walk the last three or four miles. Every time we went to teach this family it took our entire day. They did not have a phone and their work schedule was such that they could not tell us in advance when they would be home. There were no members in the area who could help us to determine if this family was going to be home. All we could do was to pray and ask God if this family would be home when we got there. I assure you that we listened very carefully to the Spirit so that we would not waste a day traveling to find no one there. When the Spirit told us that they would be there, we went and we were never disappointed.

My stake president suggested in a leadership meeting that we approach prayer as though we had just walked into the bishop's office at the church and found God the Father and His Son Jesus Christ in the room waiting for us. This is an intriguing thought. How would you respond if that happened to you? Would you lie down like you would on your bed thinking that you are too tired to kneel? Would you only want to spend one or two minutes in the office? Would you talk quickly, saying the same things you have said for years? Would you say a few things and then quickly leave the office without giving Him a chance to respond and communicate? Can you imagine the love that would be in that office? Can you feel how much He would want to talk to you and show that love? The next time you pray, think about being in that office and talk as though you were there. See if that doesn't change the way you pray.

I can testify to you that prayers are answered. I have seen it in my own life and in the lives of many others. I have seen it in the simple faith of a child and the powerful faith of someone of sage years. I will relate a brief story that will reinforce the testimony that you probably already have of prayer.

Several years ago, a man broke into our home with the intention of molesting one of my boys who was eight years old at the time. My eight-year-old and my ten-year-old slept in the same room. The man broke into the window of my daughter's room and in letting himself in, stepped on the pillow, missing my child's head by less than two inches. He crossed the hall and entered the boys' room. He stood at the foot of my younger son's bed, standing about halfway in the doorway. He woke my son and began telling him what he was going to do to him. My ten-year-old son was awakened also by the man's voice and he peeked through a hole in his blanket to see who it was that was using such filthy language. When he saw the situation, he felt like he had to do something. The man was halfway in front of the doorway but my ten-year-old decided he was going to try to run past him and get upstairs to my wife's and my bedroom and get us. He said a quick prayer and simply asked God to help him get by the man. Having said the prayer, he sat up, removed the covers and ran right past the man and up the stairs to wake us. It happened so fast that the man didn't notice until my son had run by him. The man immediately ran back through the window and left without bringing any harm to my eight-year-old.

This was a testimony of prayer for our family in two ways. Of course there was the obvious answer to the prayer of my ten-year-old by which I feel the Lord actually protected him as he had to run so close by the man in the house. Who knows what may have happened if the man had simply put his arm out and stopped him? I think that either he was concealed from the man's view or that angels escorted him out of the room.

The second testimony of prayer from that experience was that in our family prayer earlier that night, we had asked God specifically to protect us and to watch over us. Now you may think that this prayer was not answered because the man got into our house and tried to do harm to my young boy, but that is exactly why it was answered. The man tried but failed! God had protected us! You're probably curious as to what happened to the man. He was caught and ended up spending several years in prison for that crime and others he had committed.

Prayer really is the soul's sincere desire. Let it be yours and really learn to talk with God.

Now for your assignment. It is actually a three-part assignment. First, review your day in the evening and plan your day in the morning and then pray as though you were in the Lord's office and talk with Him as you would if He were there. Second, offer one prayer in which you only thank God for blessings. Don't ask for anything, just give Him thanks. Third, sometime during this week, offer a single prayer of thirty minutes or more. You will probably spend the first five minutes going through all of the things you normally go through, but you will spend the last twenty-five minutes talking with God.

Once you achieve a higher level of prayer, continue to develop it and communicate earnestly with God and you will gain an intimate relationship with Him that will serve you throughout your life.

# CHAPTER 4

# D & C SECTION 4: WHAT DOES "ALL" MEAN?

Let's take a look at the first part of Doctrine and Covenants Section 4 and see if we can tell why this section of scripture is probably the most quoted of all scriptures for missionary work.

"NOW behold, a marvelous work is about to come forth among the children of men. Therefore, O ye that embark in the service of God, see that ye serve him with **all** your heart, might, mind and strength, that ye may stand blameless before God at the last day. Therefore, if ye have desires to serve God ye are called to the work; For behold the field is white already to harvest; and lo, he that thrusteth in his sickle with his might, the same layeth up in store that he perisheth not, but bringeth salvation to his soul; And faith, hope, charity and love, with an eye single to the glory of God, qualify him for the work. Remember faith, virtue, knowledge, temperance, patience, brotherly kindness, godliness, charity, humility, diligence. Ask, and ye shall receive; knock, and it shall be opened unto you. Amen (D&C 4, highlight and underline added).

You will notice as you read the above section that I have highlighted the word all. I ask you, do you think that the Lord intended to have this word included in this section? What difference would it make to you as you read it to have that word omitted? I have noticed quite regularly in the scriptures that the Lord does not include things that are not necessary to the meaning and spirit of any given passage. There is no doubt at all in my mind that the Lord intended the word *all* to be part of this section and that it is imperative to its ultimate meaning.

But what does *all* mean in this scripture? The Lord asks those who embark in His service to serve with *all* of their heart, might, mind and strength. I would like to approach these in reverse order.

What does it mean to serve with all of your strength? What is strength? The dictionary defines it as the capacity or power for work or vigorous activity. You will truly need all of your strength in order to fulfill the requirements of your mission. Most nights you will return to your apartment exhilarated but totally exhausted. You will find that not only are you physically fatigued, but spiritually drained as well.

You will be physically spent because of the hours of hard work and the time spent riding bikes or walking to appointments, tracting, holding street meetings and all of the other physical activities that will take your time. You will find yourself spiritually overcome because of the spiritual experiences you are having or you might find that you must struggle to keep the Spirit in your area. Both can be physically draining.

If you are in an area where you are surrounded by the bad things of the world, you will have to constantly focus on the things of the Spirit in order to maintain His presence. If you are having wonderful spiritual experiences, you will find yourself sometimes almost unable to stand physically because of the effect of the Holy Ghost.

Let me give you an example or two of both situations. In my first area, we lived in a difficult part of town. The building we lived in had several tenants who enjoyed a good party. These parties only happened once every other month or so but they went on for three or four days, literally nonstop. They lived right above us and the music was always so loud that sleep was difficult. There was dancing, drugs, drinking and just general non-spiritual things going on. From time to time some of them would come down to our apartment and knock on the door at two or three in the morning and try to entice us to go up to the party. I think they were genuinely trying to be friendly in their offer, thinking that we were lonely and could use the company.

Most of the time during these parties, there were scantily-clad young women coming and going from the apartment. Of course this had a tendency to be very distracting and it really took an exhaustive amount of prayer, study and faith to maintain the Spirit during those days. Not only were we spent physically because of the normal rigors of missionary work, but we were totally drained spiritually and physically from the extra efforts made in order to maintain the Spirit!

Now let's look at how having positive spiritual experiences can take the physical strength from you. Here are a couple of examples from the scriptures.

"When the light rested upon me I saw two Personages, whose brightness and glory defy all description, standing above me in the air. One of them spake unto me, calling me by name and said, pointing to the other—This is My Beloved Son. Hear Him! My object in going to inquire of the Lord was to know which of all the sects was right, that I might know which to join. No sooner, therefore, did I get possession of myself, so as to be able to speak, than I asked the Personages who stood above me in the light, which of all the sects was right (for at this time it had never entered into my heart that all were wrong)—and which I should join. I was answered that I must join none of them, for they were all wrong; and the Personage who addressed me said that all their creeds were an abomination in his sight; that those professors were all corrupt; that 'they draw near to me with their lips, but their hearts are far from me, they teach for doctrines the commandments of men, having a form of godliness, but they deny the power thereof.' He again forbade me to join with any of them; and many other things did he say unto me, which I cannot write at this time. *When I came to myself again, I found myself lying on my back, looking up into heaven. When the light had departed, I had no strength*; but soon recovering in some degree, I went home" (Joseph Smith History 17-20, emphasis added).

"Wherefore it came to pass that my father, Lehi, as he went forth prayed unto the Lord, yea, even with all his heart, in behalf of his people. And it came to pass as he prayed unto the Lord, there came a pillar of fire and dwelt upon a rock before him; and he saw and heard much; and because of the things which he saw and heard he did quake and tremble exceedingly. And it came to pass that *he returned to his own house at Jerusalem; and he cast himself upon his bed, being overcome with the Spirit* and the things which he had seen" (1 Nephi 1: 5-7, emphasis added).

You will note that both Joseph Smith and Lehi lost their physical strength because of spiritual experiences. Although it is tiring, it is the best tired you can imagine! When you are in the mission field, you will have the opportunity to have sacred spiritual experiences every single day. It will be up to you whether or not you have them. If you do you will understand what the Lord meant when he said to serve Him will all of your strength.

Now let's look at serving with all of your mind. Think for a moment what it means to serve with all of your mind. Once again, I remind you that He did not ask for 95 percent of your mind, but all of it! If you read *Dare to Prepare*, in chapter two we discussed a little bit about mind control and how you must have total control of your mind in order to control your eternal destiny.

When you serve with all of your mind, you will have total

focus on the work of the Lord. You will of course study the appropriate things that the mission president asks you to study. You will focus on memorizing things that he will ask you to commit to memory. You will not let your mind wander from topic to topic. You will be constantly using your mind to better yourself and your companion in the work. At every door that you are approaching you will be praying in your mind and heart that the person who answers the door will listen to you. If your companion is talking, either at a door or during a discussion, you will be praying that the Spirit will communicate what is being said to the heart of the investigator. You will be bearing silent testimony by nodding your head in agreement with your companion's message. You will be totally focused. (Note that the word totally contains the word all).

When I was with the second Elder I was training, it became evident that he was letting his mind wander. When we were in discussions he would, from time to time, start cracking his knuckles! Not only was that incredibly distracting but it was obvious that he had very little interest in what was being said or if the investigators were listening. Certainly it was a simple habit that he had formed and he wasn't trying to be disruptive or rude but he needed to focus and put forth the tremendous effort needed to keep his mind on the work at hand. It is not easy! In my other book I ask you to focus on something without distraction for a period of time. It is very difficult to do but we must learn how to do it the best we can.

Another Elder I knew in the mission field had his mind on his home for a period of time. I went into a sacrament meeting and found this Elder in tears on the back row. There were still a few minutes before the meeting was to begin so I asked him if everything was OK. He responded by saying, "They cut it down." I asked him who cut what down and he said that his family had cut down the cherry tree in their yard and had mentioned it in his last letter from home. I was sure that that couldn't be the whole story and so I asked him what was bothering him about that. He responded by saying that it was the tree that he had played in when he was a little boy and that he had had a tree house in that tree and then concluded with the question, "How could they do that?" I'm certain that that tree meant a lot to this elder, but it literally took his mind off of the Lord's work for almost two weeks! You simply must learn to focus.

If you will focus on the work, you will find the Lord sending revelations to your mind that will benefit you, your companion, and those around you. You will find that the more you control your mind and give it all to the Lord, He will bless you in ways you cannot explain. You will hold your destiny in your hands if you can control your mind. After all, the Lord asked for all of your mind.

Now let's look at 'might.' What does 'all your might' mean? I can assure you it doesn't mean you might give your all! Might means the right and power to command, rule, decide or judge. Might is different than strength because it has to do with wisdom. Commanding, ruling, deciding and judging all require wisdom. Wisdom is coating your knowledge with the Spirit. You must use all of your wisdom in the Lord's work. You will make many decisions every day—where to work, what to teach, how hard to commit, what to study, etc. Every judgment you make will affect each day and potentially your entire mission. If you make the wrong decision about something, it could keep someone from entering the waters of baptism. On the other hand, the right decisions could bring them into the baptism font. Of course, the only way to make the right decision every time is to listen carefully to the Spirit and follow its promptings.

While working in one of the more difficult areas of the mission, my companion and I had one of the amazing experiences you frequently hear about from returned missionaries.

We knocked on a door and a woman answered with a huge

smile and told us she had just been on her knees begging God to send her some spiritual direction. We expressed who we were and why we were there and she asked us to come back when her husband was home. We returned that night and found him every bit as receptive as she had been. We took them to church the following Sunday and invited them to what we called the Baptismal Discussion. It was a wonderful discussion that combined all of the necessary principles of the gospel in one ninety-minute discussion. It was so complete that if an investigator had been to church and participated in this discussion, they could be baptized.

Many were baptized following this highly powerful presentation. This couple stayed after church for the discussion and were so excited they could hardly wait. They even asked us about baptism before the discussion. During the discussion there was a section about the law of chastity in which the Elder giving the discussion would talk about the sacred powers of procreation and how they are to be handled. He would ask the question, "Do you feel it would be important to live the law of chastity?" On this occasion, the Elder giving the discussion forgot how to word that question and instead asked the husband, "Have you ever broken the law of chastity?" The husband looked at the missionary in a bit of shock and didn't respond for a moment. Then he finally admitted that he had broken the law of chastity. His wife looked at him in shock, along with the other fifteen or so who were attending the discussion. After an uncomfortable moment his wife said, "I forgive you!" and told him that this would be their new start and that everything in the past would be water under the bridge. However, the husband felt so humiliated by the situation and the circumstance that he got up and left the discussion and refused to ever come back or let his wife.

We lost the most golden couple I ever came across in the mission field because of the way an Elder phrased a question.

He wasn't using wisdom when he decided to put the question the way he did. My companion and I returned to the home several times and they would never let us in again. I only hope that at some point in time they were able to find the courage to join the Saints.

On another occasion I was tracting with a leader during a companion split. The leader was anxious to demonstrate his faith and get us into several doors. He did have great faith and was very diligent. However, when we came to one door, the man behind the door invited us in and asked us to sit down for just a few minutes while the biggest sporting event in Australia was just winding up on TV. He said he would be happy to listen to us when the game was over. My companion said that our message was more important than the game and reached over and turned off the TV!! Of course, our message was far more important than the game but this man didn't know that. He had told us he would listen to our message in a few minutes and maybe then he would have understood how important our message was but he was so angry that this Elder had shut off the game just near the end that he ordered us out of his house and told us never to come back again. Turning off the TV was this Elder's way of showing me how to work with faith. I think it would have worked much better if we had agreed to come back in half an hour. I really think we might have been able to teach that man.

Be wise and give the Lord all of your might. This is a process to learn how to use wisdom in the work, but as you ask the Lord to help you and you talk things over with your companion, you will begin to see wisdom in your decisions and judgments.

Now let's look at serving with all of your heart. What does that mean? Can you serve with all of your heart if half of your heart is at home? Now I'll probably get a lot of flack for this and there are several of you who will probably stop reading this book right after you read the next sentence but I would ask you to finish the chapter and do the assignment before you drop it completely. Speaking from my own experience, I have never seen a single situation where an Elder had someone waiting for him and it helped him in the work. There, I've said it! I truly never did see a single situation where an Elder had a girlfriend at home and was able to serve with all of his heart. The word *all* doesn't leave room for much else. It is not possible to be serving the Lord with all of your heart if you spend time thinking about your girlfriend back home. I knew several Elders who thought they would be the exception, but I never saw it happen.

The second Elder I trained had a girlfriend at home and every Tuesday he would spend his study time waiting out by the mailbox for a letter. This was hard to deal with for several reasons. First, I had to go with him so he would not be alone. Second, if the letter was a few days late, we spent several days out by the mailbox during study time. During the mail strike, we went a couple of months without receiving anything at all. I thought he was going to die! Then, one day a letter came and after he read it he threw it on the bed in disgust and left the room. I thought, great, he finally got his 'Dear John' and we can get to work. When he came back in the room, it was obvious that he was depressed. I asked him what was wrong and he threw the letter to me and told me to read it. It said that things were fine at home and the she had gone to a young men/young women activity and had a fun time. She told him to work hard and to baptize and said she was praying for him. When I finished, I was confused at his depression and I asked him again what was wrong. He said, "Did you read it?" I told him I had, to which he replied, "Did you read where she went to the activity and had fun?" Again I confirmed that I had read that part, to which he replied, "There were young men there too, you know!" I could not believe that that was the cause of his depression, but it was. He remained depressed for an entire week until he got another letter that hadn't shaken him. It was a hard week for both of us because he could not concentrate on the Lord's work.

I knew many Elders who had someone at home tugging at their heart strings and who never really lost themselves in the work until that tie was broken. It always seemed like they were able to focus more clearly when there wasn't an attachment stretching from their girlfriend's house to their mission apartment. Now, don't get me wrong. You may be the one who is able to serve with all your heart while having a girlfriend (or boyfriend for you sisters) but I just have never seen it happen. Not while I was in the mission field or from any of the missionaries that have written to me in the many years that I have taught missionary preparation.

I am not making a blanket statement that you should not go into the mission field with a 'friend' waiting for you. What I am saying is that you must be careful to make sure that the relationship from home does not detract one whit from you serving with all of your heart. That doesn't mean 99 percent of your heart. The Lord asks for it all for the length of your mission! I am certain that if I had not cut all of those types of ties before I left, I would not have been able to give it all. You may have to ask your companion to tell you if they feel like you are lacking. Their perspective may be more clear than yours.

I don't want to receive hate mail or threatening phone calls from your friends. I just want you to remember that there is nothing more important during your mission experience than the Lord's work. He wants you completely for two years (or eighteen months). He wants the whole package and He wants it ALL. If you give it to Him, there will be plenty of time and opportunity for the other relationships in life afterwards.

Try this experiment. Try to focus on two things at one time. Go ahead and try right now to focus clearly on

THESE                                                    WORDS

at the same time. It isn't possible. Go to a mirror and try to look at both of your eyes at the same time. You can look at either one, but you can't look at both eyes at the same time. I really want you to go and try it. It won't take long, and as always, I promise I will be here when you get back.

Just as it is impossible to focus on two different things at the same time, so it is impossible to focus on your mission and something else at the same time. If you focus on anything else, you have lost the focus on your mission.

"And if your eye be single to my glory, your whole bodies shall be filled with light, and there shall be no darkness in you; and that body which is filled with light comprehendeth all things. Therefore, sanctify yourselves that your minds become single to God, and the days will come that you shall see him; for he will unveil his face unto you, and it shall be in his own time, and in his own way, and according to his own will. Remember the great and last promise which I have made unto you; cast away your idle thoughts . . ." (D&C 88:67-69).

What a promise! If we keep our eye single we will know all things and see God! What more could you ask than that?

Now there is one other potential trouble with your heart. I have expressed to you the need to love the people among whom you serve and I hope that you understood me to mean to love them as brothers and sisters. You must never let your heart become involved with someone you meet in the mission field, whether it be another missionary, an investigator or just someone you meet. Although it is a bit lengthy, I have included here a copy of an outstanding talk given by President Spencer W. Kimball while a member of the Quorum of the Twelve Apostles while on a Latin American Mission tour in 1968. It is entitled "Lock Your Hearts."

"If there are problems in the mission that you can give me light on so that I can help your President and help you, that's what I'd like. If there are situations that are difficult, if there are problems that are unknown - let me give you one example:

In one of the missions I found a bad situation. One or two missionaries had been breaking rules (as the President has talked about this morning). They began to break some rules. All they did was go over to a certain home every Sunday night for a dinner. The President didn't know anything about it. It wasn't very serious; they should have been home studying, but it was a regular thing every week. After a little while these missionaries were bringing others and pretty soon they were dancing on Sunday night, a few of them. Then they were doing a little flirting and then a few of them got to playing cards there every Sunday night. And then they were dancing in the dark with some of the Saint's girls!

The next thing we knew there was an excommunication. I came there and the things were revealed. I found that where there was only one boy who had actually gone to the extreme where he had to be excommunicated, there were about eighteen missionaries in this area who had followed like sheep over the ledge. They had not intended to do anything wrong, but they had just kind of followed the leadership. They had gone there to the meals—and they had gotten into little flirtations— not too deeply, but the thing is that there were eighteen missionaries who knew that this boy had gone too far. They knew that he was necking and petting but not one of them would ever tell! When I interviewed them and visited with them I said, "Why didn't you tell the President that conditions were bad?" One of them said, "Well, that's none of my business! This Elder can do as he pleases! If he wants to wreck his mission, that's okay with me, it's his business, it's his mission! If he wants to ruin his life that's up to him. It's his life!!"

And then I said to these Elders, "Well what about your missions? Isn't this your mission, too? Isn't this your church, too? Are you willing that one person nullify all that you've done here? You've spent twenty months down here, Elder, and you have been working reasonably hard and at times you have done remarkably good work. Are you willing that one scandal—one scandal in this out-of-the-world place—will neutralize all that you've done? All of your efforts? That's what happens! Are you willing to do that?" He said, "Well I hadn't thought of it like that." Well, but that's what happened, isn't it, Elders? This is your mission! This is your church! One scandal in a community is enough to annihilate the work of all of you, maybe all the work you do cumulatively—for all your two years—neutralized by one scandal in the community! Do you think that you have a loyalty? Where are your loyalties? Are you loyal to yourself? Are you loyal to your companion? Are you willing to let him go on, and on, and on, and on, until he breaks his neck?

When he was excommunicated it was a sad day in that mission because he was a fine young man and all the missionaries loved him, and some of them were weeping that day. I remember! Some of them were weeping tears! Their brother was being excommunicated from the Church and sent home in disgrace!

And then I said to them, "Elders! Do you know who excommunicated this boy? Not me; not your president; not the Elder's court. It was you!! You excommunicated your brother! How? Well, if you'd have said, 'Elder, lets not do that! That disturbs our whole program. We lose spirituality, all of us, when things like this happen.' Now suppose that he didn't yield and you said to him again, 'Elder, you shouldn't do that! We can't be doing those kinds of things!' And then suppose you'd gone a third time and said, 'Elder, I'm sorry, if you don't desist I'm going to have to report to the mission president because I'm not going to have you destroy my work! I've worked too hard to have it all go to the wind! I'm going to tell the president, not as a tattletale, but I'm going to report to the president so that he can protect the whole program, if you don't desist!'"

You see there is nothing ugly about that, is there? That's the way it should be because our loyalty is first to the Lord, to the Church, to the mission, to the world, isn't it?

One more little incident that is connected: In one United States mission one day a neighbor came into the home of a new member. The neighbor was not a member, but she came and she was used to just walking in through the door—you know, she didn't always knock! So she came over to this home this day and she saw her friend, the Latter-day Saint sister, sitting on a chair here and an Elder at her feet—this will shock you—trimming her toe-nails or painting her toe-nails, or something! Well, now that isn't an unpardonable sin, but it was indiscreet, wasn't it? Even if there was nothing else that happened, just the fact that he was sitting on the floor and that he didn't have on his tie and coat, and here was a woman partly dressed, and here he was painting her toe-nails or doing something! Anyway, that city was closed, absolutely closed to missionary work for twenty years! Do you think missionaries could go in that city? Why of course they couldn't! Because there was still the memory of this indiscretion! They hadn't committed sin; at least, I'm quite sure he had never committed immorality. I think it wasn't any more than an ugly indiscretion. It was ugly enough, wasn't it? It was what it led to, you see?

That's why I say this mission belongs to you. There are 150 of you and this mission belongs to all of you. If anything happens to any part of this mission it gets a black eye! It makes it more difficult to do anything! And it makes it more difficult for you to go into the homes where they have heard ugly things about the Church. That's why one Elder isn't by himself. He can't be a loner. He has got to fit into the program, hasn't he? And everyone of you is interested. Everyone!! And you can't afford to let your companion, or anyone you know, do anything very serious because it all brings trouble to you and to the whole program. Well, think about that a little, because some people say, "I'm not going to be a stool pigeon! I'm not going to tattle! I'm not going to be telling on people!" It isn't that at all! It's a reporting just like if you saw a couple of robbers going into your neighbor's home. Would you say, "Well, it's up to them! It's up to my neighbors!" No!! We'd become involved! We'd rush to the telephone, we'd call the police! In every case, wouldn't we?

If we saw somebody being injured, being killed—like in New York sometime ago, a girl was stabbed and cut all to pieces by some maniac, and there were many people who saw it and did nothing about it! She yelled for help, screamed for help, said, "He's killing me!!" But nobody would move! They didn't even call the police and there she lay, finally dead, on the street! Nobody would involve themselves. It's time we would begin to get involved when involvement is proper. And when any missionary in any mission begins to break mission rules, it's time that all his companions should become involved! It doesn't mean that they take over. It doesn't mean that they get ugly and mean. It just means that they are interested and involved. There is a nice way to do it! I tell you there wouldn't

61

be very many broken rules if one missionary would just say to the other, "Brother, lets not do that! Let's don't do that! Let's don't stand there and talk to those girls! That isn't good!" And if we stop it when it's fresh—when it's young you can stop it—but when it gets deeply entrenched, that sin is awfully hard to dig out. And many times we have to send missionaries home to their families in disgrace, with excommunication frequently, because maybe their companions didn't love them enough! Maybe their companions weren't helpful enough to say, "Well, now, you're getting off the line just a little here! Let's don't do that! Let's get busy and do this, and this, and this!"

This is one program and we are all concerned about it. These mission rules, you see, are very important. We've had 137 years of experience. Now that ought to be enough experience to prove something, shouldn't it?

Through 137 years we have come to the conclusion that if two people will stay together the chances for sin or serious trouble are reduced about 98 percent. Once in a great while two companions will both go sour at the same time, but it isn't the usual thing. If missionaries will, when they leave Salt Lake City, the mission home—the day they are set apart—if they will just lock their hearts! If they've got a girl in there, that's all right, lock her in! But if you haven't got one in, then lock it against all other girls of every description! And the same applies for young women, too. I am talking mainly to you Elders. You lock your heart and leave the key at home. And you never open it here! It's impossible to fall in love with someone unless you open your heart! Your heart is the only organ that has any ability to get into love, you see, and when a missionary says, "I just fell in love with a girl!" Well, that's as silly as it can be! Nobody does, nobody ever did!

So we just don't fall in love unless we are fooling around.

We never fall in a crater unless we are somewhere near the edge of it. I have been up to Vesuvius and on a number of craters and volcanoes and I know you just don't ever fall in a crater unless you are on the edge of it. And so you just keep your hearts locked! I said lock them in Salt Lake when you leave the mission home and don't give a thought to it. But if you go around and say, "Well, she is kind of a pretty girl! She surely is a sweet little thing! She's a nice girl! I'd like to talk to her— I'd just like to visit with her!" Well, you are in for trouble and that trouble can bring you a lifetime of trouble and a lifetime of regrets if you continue on with it.

So, can I impress that again? LOCK YOUR HEARTS and leave the key at home! Wherever you live, leave the key home with your folks. And your heart—it's only that part of it that deals with people generally that you open up. We just can't tolerate it, can we? We can't individually; we can't totally. Someone said, "Well, is there any harm to marry a Mexican girl if you are working in Mexico!" No, that isn't any crime, but it proves that some missionary has had his heart open! He has unlocked it! Is it wrong to marry a German girl when you have been on a German mission? Why no, there is no crime in that, if you met her some other way. But when you meet her in the mission field and you have opened your heart, I tell you it isn't right, and you have shortchanged your mission! Just keep your hearts locked. Your whole thought should be missionary work. How can I make it more plain and more important than that? I'd like to because there is no reason whatever for any missionary to ever become involved, not even in a decent way, with any girl in the mission field. It isn't the place! You guaranteed, you promised! You went through the temple! You remember what you did in the temple? Remember you promised you'd do all the things the brethren request of you, to live the commandments. That's one of the commandments

63

when you go into the mission field: "Thou shalt not flirt! Thou shalt not associate with young women in the mission field—or anyone else for that matter—on any other basis than the proselyting basis." You promised, and you would not want to break a promise you made before the Lord in the holy temple of the Lord. And when you wrote the letter of acceptance to President McKay, that was implied in it. You knew of course—every missionary knows—that he isn't going out to court, that he isn't going out to find a wife! He's got plenty of opportunity when he gets home, and the mission field isn't the place.

Sometimes we find a young man who has not been popular at home; he has been very, very backward at home and he hasn't had many dates. So when he gets out into the mission field and somebody flatters him a little—some girl shows a lot of interest in him—why he's flattered. He thinks all at once, "Well, that's whom I should marry!" Well, I say this once more by repetition and for emphasis, you LOCK YOUR HEARTS and if you haven't done so, do it now and send the key back! You will not permit any impression, no romantic thought or impression in your mind. For two years you have given yourself to the Lord, totally, to teach the gospel to the world. When you have done this perfectly for two years and then you go home, you are infinitely more attractive, more able, more dignified, more mature to make those important decisions for your life in the matter of personages to enjoy eternity with you.

Well, I didn't intend to get on to that, either, but I've been on it, and I hope I have not been offensive in it at all. I hope you got the spirit of it. Should you know of any problems that are aborning, problems that are beginning to develop, some missionary who is getting off the track, some group that is getting a little careless about mission rules, you can talk to them in a sweet kindly way. If they persist, then there is something else to do and you have a loyalty to it.

God bless you missionaries and I hope to visit with you a little longer later" (Spencer W. Kimball).

Remember that "To every thing there is a season, and a time to every purpose under the heaven" (Ecclesiastes 3:1). The time for proper courting and relationships will come, but for now, the Lord needs you!

The promise of Section 4 is that if you give it all, you will stand blameless before God at the last day! That is an amazing promise, to stand blameless before God at the last day as far as you mission is concerned.

Now if you have something else on your mind so you don't use wise judgment or your heart is elsewhere or you don't give it all your strength, there is no promise as to you remaining blameless. I know that during the "week of depression" with my companion that we were not as effective as we could have been and we may have missed someone we should have asked a golden question on the street because my companion's mind was otherwise occupied. If we just passed one person because of his distraction that we should have contacted, we could have missed the chance to have influenced dozens of lives by now and thousands more in the generations to follow. How could we remain blameless having missed an opportunity like that when we could have done something to change the situation?

Now for your assignment. Don't worry, I am not going to tell you to cut off your relationships. What I am going to ask you to do is to discuss it with Heavenly Father—He who knows all things and will give you the proper direction. If there is someone who you are dating, ask them to join with you in possibly fasting and prayer so you will know what you need to do in order to be able to give it all.

Ask God to bless you with the abilities needed to give it all in all four categories - heart, might, mind and strength. Let him know how anxious you are to be the best missionary you can be and ask him to give you specific abilities and guidance. Once you receive the response (use the steps in prayer from the previous chapter) have the courage to follow it no matter what it is and you will find His hand in your life and see it in your mission.

# CHAPTER 5

# TWO THINGS TO REMOVE FROM YOUR "THINGS TO DO" LIST

Like most missionaries, you probably have a list of the many things you need to do in order to get ready for your mission. This list might include things like: Buy a suit, buy several pairs of garments, buy several pairs of socks, meet with the Stake President, finish the Book of Mormon before you meet with the Stake President, etc.

Granted, there are a seemingly a million things to do in order to get ready for your mission. Everything from reading books to help you prepare to getting a hair cut to finding comfortable shoes.

However, there are two items that show up on most "missionary preparation" lists that I hope would not be there. The two items are—First, go to the temple for your endowments and second, obtain a patriarchal blessing.

Now don't get me wrong. I certainly hope that you have a strong desire to receive both of these wonderful gifts. And that is why I hope they are not on your list. I hope that you do not need to rely on a list to remind you to participate in these two incredible opportunities. These two items are of such great importance that you should not have to be reminded at all.

Let's look for a moment at both of these wonderful items and see why they should be so important to us that having them on a list would be useless because we wouldn't need to be reminded to do them. The things that we strongly desire are constantly on our minds and don't require inclusion on a to-do list.

What if you went out into your mail box today and found a letter like this addressed to you?

**Elohim—Your Eternal Father**
**Heaven**

> Prepaid
> Priority
> Mail

*Personal!!*

**Your Name Here**
**Your Address Here**
**Your City, State, and Zip Here**

How would you respond to it? Now I want you to really think what you would do. Would you take it in the house and toss it on the kitchen table or on your dresser and think to yourself, "I'll look at it when I have time." Or maybe, "I've got so much to do, I'll let it sit there until I notice it again in a few weeks." Or would you immediately open it before you even got into the house to see what God sent to you? I hope that you would be so anxious to see what He had sent to you that you couldn't wait to open it and see.

That is what it is like to get a patriarchal blessing. It is as though you received a personal letter from God. I hope that you are excited enough to see what He has to say to you that you would go out of your way to get it and read it.

Let's take a look at patriarchal blessings. A couple of chapters ago, we discussed the principle of prayer. We talked about it being a problem for us to do all of the talking when we have a discussion with God. Although that is a problem when we are doing the talking, it is not a problem at all when God is doing the talking.

What a fantastic thing to receive a letter from someone who knows us so much better than we know ourselves that He can tell exactly how we will respond to anything. Knowing everything about us, He can give us His specific thoughts on our future lives. He can express to us the things we have the potential to accomplish and what we have been and might be called to do if we remain faithful. Through a righteous patriarch, God can give us direction and tell us what might be.

A patriarchal blessing is not a fortune telling type of experience. It's not from some psychic, it is from a God who knows all and sees all. It comes through a chosen servant who was called to be a representative of God.

I read once where a man called a psychic hotline and when the psychic got on the phone she asked for his credit card number. He immediately responded with, "You mean you don't know it?" and hung up. God really does know everything. The following is from a talk given June 1, 1980 at Brigham Young University by Elder Bruce R. McConkie entitled "The Seven Deadly Heresies."

Heresy one: There are those who say that God is progressing in knowledge and is learning new truths.

This is false–utterly, totally, and completely. There is not one sliver of truth in it. It grows out of a wholly twisted and incorrect view of the King Follett Sermon and of what is meant by eternal progression.

God progresses in the sense that his kingdoms increase and his dominions multiply–not in the sense that he learns new truths and discovers new laws. God is not a student. He is not a laboratory technician. He is not postulating new theories on the basis of past experiences. He has indeed graduated to that state of exaltation that consists of knowing all things and having all power . . . Why anyone should suppose that an infinite and eternal being who has presided in our universe for almost 2,555,000,000 years [see letter from W. W. Phelps, to William Smith, Times and Seasons 5:757-758], who made the sidereal heavens, whose creations are more numerous than the particles of the earth, and who is aware of the fall of every sparrow—why anyone would suppose that such a being has more to learn and new truths to discover in the laboratories of eternity is totally beyond my comprehension.

Will he one day learn something that will destroy the plan of salvation and turn man and the universe into an uncreated nothingness? Will he discover a better plan of salvation than the one he has already given to men in worlds without number?

The saving truth, as revealed to and taught, formally and officially, by the Prophet Joseph Smith in the Lectures on Faith is that God is omnipotent, omniscient, and omnipresent. He knows all things, He has all power, and He is everywhere present by the power of His Spirit. And unless we know and believe this doctrine we cannot gain faith unto life and salvation . . .

The perfections of God are named as "the perfections which belong to all of the attributes of His nature," which is to say that God possesses and has all knowledge, all faith or power, all justice, all judgment, all mercy, and all truth. He is indeed the very embodiment and personification and source of all these attributes. Does anyone suppose that God can be more honest than He already is? Neither need any suppose there are truths He does not know or knowledge He does not possess.

Thus Joseph Smith taught, and these are his words:

"Without the knowledge of all things, God would not be able to save any portion of his creatures; for it is by reason of the knowledge which He has of all things, from the beginning to the end, that enables Him to give that understanding to His creatures by which they are made partakers of eternal life; and if it were not for the idea existing in the minds of men that God had all knowledge it would be impossible for them to exercise faith in Him" (As quoted by Bruce R. McConkie in Mormon Doctrine [Salt Lake City: Bookcraft, 1966], pg. 264).

Let there be no doubt that God really does know everything from the beginning to the end. He knows everything about you and He knows exactly where you will be after this life. Not because you are predestined to be there, but because He knows you so well that He knows exactly how you will respond to everything in your life. He even knows that you are reading this book and He knows what you are thinking about while you are reading.

Of course He can direct a worthy patriarch to give you a blessing that will describe things that are in your future if you are righteous.

My mother told me once that her father, who was a member of the Quorum of the Twelve Apostles, told her that whenever he had the privilege of calling a new patriarch, the Lord made the new man's face very familiar to him so that he would know the face when he attended stake conference. All he had to do was to find the face he had seen. He said that the revelation he received in calling a patriarch was much more direct and clear than when calling anyone else to any position.

Now you may well find that the things found in your blessing will take place in your life on many levels. You may find something in your blessing fulfilled several times. For example, you may be told that you will serve the Lord in the capacity of a missionary. Then you will go on your mission and serve Him and think that that part was fulfilled. Later in life you might serve as a ward missionary and think that that part was fulfilled again. Later still, you and your spouse might have the blessing of serving as couple missionaries and again you would think that the blessing was fulfilled. You may be called upon on the other side of the veil to do even more missionary work and see yet another fulfillment of your blessing.

If you read *Dare To Prepare*, in the chapter on study, there was a grid of squares and we talked about getting the deeper meaning out of the scriptures. (If you haven't read it, go and get it and look at that chapter). Your patriarchal blessing is quite literally personal scripture for you. It is your own chapter of sacred scripture and you will find as you read it over and over again that the meaning will deepen and you will see things that you never saw before.

I try to make it a habit to read my patriarchal blessing on fast Sunday. It helps me to remember to read it often and when I approach it while in the mode of fasting and prayer, I feel I get more out of it.

Of course, being personal scripture for you and only you, it is a good idea to keep it to yourself unless prompted by the spirit to share it with someone else. I can count on one hand how many people I have allowed to read my blessing. It is very sacred to me and was given to me for my personal use.

Some blessings are short, some are long—how can they be from the same God if they are so different in tone and structure? I know friends whose blessings are several pages in length and others whose blessings are only a half of a page long. Is it because one person is more in tune than another? Is it because the patriarch is out of touch so he gives a short one?

If you look at the scriptures, you will find that the writers all have different styles. Some write things in a more lengthy fashion and some are very brief. For example, in the Book of Mormon, the first two books, written by Nephi, take a total of fifty-five chapters. In contrast, the "Book" of Chemish is only one verse in length. Don't worry if your blessing is long or short. It doesn't matter. What does matter is that the Lord will speak personally to you about your life.

Several years ago, it used to be the practice to obtain multiple patriarchal blessings. My maternal grandparents each had several. They would go through their lives for several years and then think that they wanted more direction so they would go and receive another one.

That is no longer the case. We basically get one per customer, but that is enough. If you will cherish it and read it often, you will see God's hand in your life, not only in the mission field, but in every moment thereafter as well. You should be so anxious to get your blessing, if you don't already have it, that you should not need a reminder on a list to get it done.

Now let's talk about the second item that should not be on your to-do list—going to the temple.

Here is another item that you might find in your mail box.

---

*You are invited to come to a special*

## Study Group

*Where:* **The House of the Lord**

*When:* **Anytime you would like**

*Please RSVP:* **Your Bishop and your Stake President**

**Please come prepared to learn the necessary things to return to God's presence, dwell with Him and his Son and have all that they have.**

---

What an opportunity to be invited to the literal House of the Lord and learn from His spirit the things that will help us to enter His presence! The temple is His house in every sense of the word. I am convinced that He visits his temples and has walked their halls and touched their walls. The temple is not only His house but His university as well.

In order to qualify to enter His house there are certain requirements. When you interview with the bishop and the stake president you will find that they will ask you the same questions. They will try to asses your worthiness to enter into the Lord's house and receive your endowment. You will be asked if you have a testimony of the gospel, support local and General Authorities, attend your meetings, accept and follow the teachings and programs of the Church, keep the Word of Wisdom, pay a full tithing, are honest, are morally clean (free from adultery, fornication, and homosexuality, etc.), are a member in good standing in the Church and if you feel you are worthy to enter the Lord's house and participate in His ordinances.

If you answer every question honestly and completely and you are issued a recommend, you can be sure that you are worthy to enter the Lord's house. You will notice that the bishop and stake president don't give you a ticket or a pass; they give you a recommend. They recommend you to the Lord in His house. Are you as excited about getting your recommend as you would be about getting the invitation to go to the Lord's house?

In the temple, you will learn many important things. They are so important that a man cannot enter the Celestial Kingdom who has not had the privilege of receiving the blessings of the temple. You must receive your own endowment and you must be sealed in the temple in order to dwell where God dwells. Brigham young said . . .

"Let me give you a definition in brief. Your endowment is to receive all those ordinances in the house of the Lord, which are necessary for you, after you have departed this life, to enable you to walk back to the presence of the Father, passing the angels who stand as sentinels, being enabled to give them the key words, the signs and tokens, pertaining to the holy Priesthood, and gain your eternal exaltation in spite of earth and hell" (Discourses of Brigham Young [Deseret Book Co., 1941], p. 416).

Elder James E. Talmage said . . .

"The Temple Endowment, as administered in modern temples, comprises instruction relating to the significance and sequence of past dispensations, and the importance of the present as the greatest and grandest era in human history. This course of instruction includes a recital of the most prominent events of the creative period, the condition of our first parents in the Garden of Eden, their disobedience and consequent expulsion from that blissful abode, their condition in the lone and dreary world when doomed to live by labor and sweat, the plan of redemption by which the great transgression may be atoned, the period of the great apostasy, the restoration of the Gospel with all its ancient powers and privileges, the absolute and indispensable condition of personal purity and devotion to the right in present life, and a strict compliance with Gospel requirements . . .

"The ordinances of the endowment embody certain obligations on the part of the individual, such as covenant and promise to observe the law of strict virtue and chastity, to be charitable, benevolent, tolerant and pure; to devote both talent and material means to the spread of truth and the uplifting of the race; to maintain devotion to the cause of truth; and to seek in every way to contribute to the great preparation that the earth may be made ready to receive her King—the Lord Jesus Christ. With the taking of each covenant and the assuming of each obligation a promised blessing is pronounced, contingent upon the faithful observance of the conditions.

"No jot, iota, or tittle of the temple rites is otherwise than uplifting and sanctifying. In every detail the endowment ceremony contributes to covenants of morality of life, consecration of person to high ideals, devotion to truth, patriotism to nation, and allegiance to God" (The House of the Lord [Deseret Book Co., 1968], pp. 83-84).

You will notice when you go to the temple that it is virtually impossible to tell a rich man from a poor one. All are dressed similarly in white. White reminds us of the purity of the temple and everyone dressing basically the same reminds us that we are all equal in God's sight.

Going to the temple and receiving your endowment is far more important than going on your mission. Let me say that again—going to the temple and receiving your endowment is far more important than going on your mission! Now if you have read the book *Dare To Prepare*, you know how important I think it is to go on a mission! But again I say that it is far more important to go to the temple and receive your endowment than it is to go on a mission.

If you don't go on a mission, you can still become exalted. If you don't receive your endowments, you cannot. It is that simple. Going to the temple is one of the five things that you must do to enter God's kingdom: baptism, confirmation, priesthood, endowment, sealing.

I hope that it is so important to you that you do not need it to be on a to-do list to make sure it gets done.

Now for your assignment. If you haven't yet received your patriarchal blessing, talk to your bishop about it and if you both feel right about it, get a recommend and go and get it. If you have received it already, get it out and read it several times during the week. See if you don't find something there that you did not see before. Do the same thing about the temple. Talk to your bishop and see when the time is right and then go and return frequently to the House of the Lord. Go as many times as you can before you enter the mission field. You will probably have many questions after the first few times you go. That is normal and shows that you are thinking about what is going on. Remember that you can ask a member of the temple presidency any questions you have, and if they know the answer, they will tell you. The more times you go, the more questions you can have answered and the more you will learn.

# CHAPTER 6

# PERFORMING PRIESTHOOD ORDINANCES

"God's decrees, his laws and commandments, the statutes and judgments that issue from him, are called his ordinances . . . Among his laws and commandments, the Lord has provided certain rites and ceremonies which are also called ordinances. These ordinance-rites might be pictured as a small circle within the larger circle of ordinance-commandments.[1]

There are many ordinances which involve the priesthood. Some of them include the following:

1. Baptism for the dead
2. Celestial marriage
3. Washing of feet
4. Endowments
5. Patriarchal blessings
6. Sacrifice
7. Washings
8. Anointings
9. Sealings
10. Naming and blessing of children
11. Baptism
12. Confirming and bestowing the Gift of the Holy Ghost
13. Sacrament
14. Conferring priesthood and ordaining to an office
15. Consecration of oil
16. Administering to the sick
17. Dedication of graves

18. Father's blessing on children
19. Blessing of comfort and council
20. Dedication of homes
21. Dusting of feet

You can see just by looking at the list that the purpose of the priesthood is to bless others.

We will herein review only the last twelve ordinances on the list. The others are reserved for the temple or are discussed in another part of this book.

How much do we know about these ordinances? For instance, do we remember how many of them start by addressing our Heavenly Father in Prayer?

Four— *Blessing of Children* (because the child has no name when we begin the ordinance)

*Consecration of Oil* (because there is no person involved)

*Dedication of Graves* (because there is no person involved)

*Dedication of Homes* (because there is no person involved)

How many of them are at least in part fixed prayers?

Three—*Baptism* (fixed from D&C 20:73)

*Sacrament blessings* (fixed from D&C 20: 77,79 with the use of the word water instead of wine)

*Confirmation and Bestowal of the Holy Ghost* (here the only portion that is necessarily fixed are the words "Receive the Holy Ghost")

## Naming and Blessing of Children

Are there any special allowances made for either nonmember or inactive fathers in association with this ordinance?

No, it used to be that fathers could hold their child when he or she is blessed whether the father was a worthy holder of the proper priesthood or not. This is no longer the case.

Is the naming and blessing of children a priesthood ordinance?

Yes, but it is not an ordinance of salvation because children are saved in the kingdom of God.[2]

What is the process of blessing and naming one of our children?[3]

A. We take them in our arms (or if they are older, place our hands upon their heads).
B. Address our Heavenly Father as in prayer.
C. State authority (Melchizedek Priesthood) by which the ordinance is being performed.
D. Give the child a name.
  1. When the child has been given a name you can give the child a blessing because now they have a name by which you can call them.
E. Add such words of blessing as the spirit dictates.
  1. Note that a blessing is directed at the child and spoken as speaking to the child, not praying to Heavenly Father. For example, you would say we bless you with . . . not, we ask Heavenly Father to bless you with . . . Once the child has a name, the ordinance which began as a prayer continues as a blessing.
F. Close in the name of Jesus Christ.

# Baptism

Who can perform the ordinance of baptism?

Anyone who is worthy and holds the office of Priest or any office in the Melchizedek Priesthood.[4]

What is the procedure to follow in baptizing someone?[5]

A. Stand in the water with the person to be baptized.

    1. If possible, make sure that you have enough water and that it is warm.

B. It is suggested that a good way to balance the weight of the one being baptized is to hold the person's right wrist in your left hand, and then have the person hold your left wrist with his left hand.

C. Raise your right arm to the square.

    1. The importance of using the right side portions of the body in the performing of ordinances began long ago and is substantiated by the scriptures. When Abraham sent a servant to find a wife for his son Isaac he made the servant place his right hand under Abraham's thigh and swear a promise.[6] When Jacob blessed his grandsons Manessah and Ephraim, he moved his hands "wittingly" in order to place his right hand on the head of Ephraim.[7] When the Egyptians were drowned in the sea, Israel raised up their voices and said, "Thy right hand, O Lord is becoming glorious in power: Thy right hand O Lord hath dashed in pieces the enemy . . ."[8] For more of a scriptural base on the right side being important see the following: Isaiah 41:10,13; 48:12-13; Psalm 110:1; Matthew 22:44; 25:31-46; 26:63-64; Acts 7:55. The right hand is also to be used when partaking of the sacrament.[9]

D. Call the individual by his full name.

E. State the baptismal prayer (D&C 20:73)

F. Place your right hand high on the person's back. Let him hold his nose with his right hand if he wishes. Completely immerse him.

G. Help the person come up out of the water.

    1. Note that a specific grip or the holding of the nose is not necessarily part of the ordinance.

# Confirmation and Bestowal of the Holy Ghost

If there is a large group participating in this ordinance, which hand is to be placed on the recipient's head?

The right hand is to be used.[10]

Does it matter on which shoulder your other hand is placed?

It doesn't matter.[11]

What is the proper procedure to follow in the confirmation process?[12]

A. Lay your hands on the head of the person to be confirmed.

B. Call the person by his or her full name.

C. State the authority (Melchizedek Priesthood) by which the ordinance is performed.

D. Confirm the person a member of The Church of    Jesus Christ of Latter-day Saints.

E. Bestow the Holy Ghost by saying to the person being confirmed: "RECEIVE THE HOLY GHOST."    (Not - RECEIVE YE)

F. Add such words of blessing as the spirit dictates.

G. Close in the name of Jesus Christ.

# Sacrament

Is there a certain posture required of the person blessing the sacrament?

Yes, he should be kneeling.[13]

If you make a mistake in the words of the blessing must you repeat the entire blessing?

No. The Church has said that if there is a mistake made, you must simply correct it. If the prayer is completed without the correction of an error, the bishop should request that the prayer be said over again correctly.

What is the procedure to follow in blessing the bread and water?[14]

A. Blessing on the bread: Kneel and say the prayer in D&C 20:77

B. Blessing on the water: Kneel and say the prayer in D&C 20:79 using the word water instead of wine.

## Conferring the Priesthood and Ordaining to an Office

Can a priest ordain another priest?

Yes but only when there is not an Elder present.[15]

Who can ordain individuals to the other offices in the Priesthood?

Anyone who is worthy and holds at least the same office in the priesthood, except teachers and deacons.[16]

Who then has the right to set apart the President of the Church?

The combined members of the twelve have the right to set him apart. They do not need to ordain him because he already holds the keys.[17]

Are keys in the priesthood given when someone is given priesthood?

No. Keys are given when someone is set apart as a president in a calling within the priesthood.[18] The keys of presidency are given by someone who has the keys of presidency to those who are set apart as presidents.[19] For example, a stake president, who has keys as a president can set apart an elders quorum president and give him keys because the stake president has keys. If a counselor in the stake presidency set the elders quorum president apart, he should not give him keys because, as a counselor, he has none to give.

What process is involved in ordaining someone to the priesthood?[20]

A. Lay your hands on the person's head.

B. Call the person by his full name.

C. State the authority (Melchizedek or Aaronic Priesthood) by which the ordinance is performed.

D. Unless it has previously been conferred, confer the Melchizedek or Aaronic Priesthood.

E. Ordain to the specific office in the priesthood, and bestow all rights, powers, and authority pertaining to the office.

F. Then, set them apart for their specific calling if there is one for them (and give them keys if you are a president and are setting them apart as a president).

G. Add such words of blessing as the Spirit dictates.

H. Close in the name of Jesus Christ.

## Consecrating Oil

Is it necessary to use olive oil or will anything else do?

Olive oil should be used! There are many references to its use in the scriptures and to its sacredness. Olive trees, branches, leaves, and oil have been treated with great care in the scriptures.[21] President Joseph Fielding Smith said: "No other kind of oil will do in anointing. It is very apparent that oil from animal flesh would never do, and there is no other kind of oil that is held so sacredly and is more suited to the anointing than the oil of olive; moreover, the Lord has placed his stamp of approval on it."[22]

How many priesthood holders are needed to consecrate oil?

One worthy priesthood holder can do it alone.[23]

What is the process involved in consecrating oil?[24]

A.  Obtain a good grade of olive oil.

B.  Hold the open container of olive oil.

C.  Address our Heavenly Father as in prayer.

D.  State the authority (Melchizedek Priesthood) by which the oil is consecrated.

E.  Consecrate the oil (not the container), and set it apart for the blessing and anointing of the sick and afflicted.

　　1.  It is very easy to accidentally consecrate the container and it is a common mistake. It is usually made by saying something like "please bless this bottle of oil" or "please bless this container of oil." These phrases sound fine but in reality they are asking a blessing on the bottle or the container. The proper language would be something like "please bless this oil."

F.  Close in the name of Jesus Christ.

## Administering to the Sick

Who can assist in administering to the sick if two Melchizedek Priesthood holders are not available?

An Aaronic Priesthood holder, a faithful non-priesthood holder, or a woman may assist in faith and in the laying on of hands with one Melchizedek Priesthood holder who is performing the administration.[25]

Can one Melchizedek Priesthood holder perform both the anointing and the sealing of the anointing in one session?

Yes. All should be done that can be done to use two worthy priesthood holders but if only one worthy priesthood holder is available, he has the authority to do both things by himself.[26]

Should the affected portion of the body be anointed with olive oil?

No. The anointing should be done at the crown of the head.[27]

What is the process involved with the administering of the sick?[28]

This ordinance is to be done in two distinct parts.

A.  Anointing

    1.  Anoint the head of the sick person using a    small amount of oil.

        a.  As mentioned earlier, the crown of the head is the proper location on which to place the oil. If the illness makes using the crown of the head impossible, use an area as close to the crown as feasible (the forehead for instance).

    2.  Lay your hands on the person's head.

    3.  Call the person by name.

    4.  State the authority (Melchizedek Priesthood)    by which the ordinance is performed.

    5.  State that you are anointing with consecrated    oil.

    6.  Close in the name of Jesus Christ.

B. Sealing the Anointing

    1.  Lay your hands on the head of the sick person.

    2.  Call the sick person by name.

    3.  State the authority (Melchizedek Priesthood) by which the ordinance is performed.

    4.  Seal the anointing that has already taken place.

    5.  Add such words of blessing as the Spirit dictates.

    6.  Close in the name of Jesus Christ.

# Dedicating Graves

Does anyone need to approve a Melchizedek Priesthood holder before he can dedicate a grave site?

Yes. He must be approved by the bishop after consulting with the family.[29]

Is the dedication of a grave site a saving ordinance of the gospel?

No. It is performed for the comfort, consolation, and

encouragement of the Saints.[30]

What is the process involved?[31]

A. Address our Heavenly Father as in prayer.

B. State the authority (Melchizedek Priesthood) by which the ordinance is performed.

C. Dedicate and consecrate the burial plot as the resting place for the body of the person who died.

    1. Note not to use the term final resting place because it is not the final place (the resurrection is for all).

    2. Use the deceased person's full name.[32]

D. Pray to the Lord, if the Spirit prompts you to do so, that this spot of earth may be hallowed and protected until the time the body is resurrected and reunited with the spirit.

E. Ask the Lord to comfort the family, and add such words of comfort as the Spirit dictates.

F. Close in the name of Jesus Christ.

# Father's Blessing on Children

Can a father give a patriarchal blessing to his children?

Yes. He can act as the natural patriarch to his household if he has accepted the new and everlasting covenant of marriage.[33]

Can a father declare the lineage of the child that he is giving a patriarchal blessing to?

Yes. He can if he is so inspired.[34]

Are father's blessings recorded in the archives of the Church whether or not the child's lineage is declared?

No. They may be recorded in family records but whether lineage is declared or not they are not recorded in the Church archives.[35]

What is the procedure for giving a regular father's blessing?[36]

A. Lay your hands on the head of the person to be blessed.

B. Call the person by his or her full name.

C. State the authority (Melchizedek Priesthood) by which blessing is given.

D. Give such words of thanks, counsel, exhortation, blessing promises as the Spirit dictates.

    1. These blessings might be appropriate if a child is leaving home for military service, school, or missions etc.

E. Close in the name of Jesus Christ.

# Blessings of Comfort and Counsel

Does a Melchizedek Priesthood holder need to be called upon in order to give a blessing of comfort or counsel?

No. He may, on special occasions, respond to his own initiative.[37]

What type of circumstances would justify a blessing of comfort or counsel?

Times of stress, trial, mental difficulty, emotional or physical problems, a death in the family, or in preparation for a stay in the hospital.[38]

Are there times when blessings of comfort or counsel should not be given?

Yes. There are some times when it would be best for an individual to work out their own problems without a blessing. There is no set rule besides reliance on the Spirit of the Lord.[39]

What is the usual procedure for giving this kind of blessing?[40]

A. Lay your hands on the head of the person to be blessed.

B. Call the person by their full name.

C. State the authority (Melchizedek Priesthood) by which the blessing is being given.

D. Give such words of thanks, counsel, exhortation, blessing, promises as the Spirit dictates.

E. Close in the name of Jesus Christ.

# Dedication of Homes

Can you dedicate a home that you still have an outstanding mortgage on or an apartment that you do not own?

Yes. A home may be dedicated as a sanctuary where family members can find safety from the world and grow spiritually in preparation for eternal family relationships.[41]

Should a home be dedicated and consecrated to the Lord?

No. Unlike Church buildings, homes should not be dedicated and consecrated to the Lord.[42]

What is the normal procedure in the dedication of a home.[43]

The procedure is not specified but it is suggested that a priesthood holder might gather his family together and offer a special prayer that would include the things mentioned above, or use any other appropriate words.

# Dusting off your Feet

In Biblical times as well as in this dispensation, the Lord has directed those who are taking the gospel to the world to perform this ordinance as a testimony against those who reject them and their message. "And whosoever shall not receive you, nor hear your words, when ye depart out of that house or city, shake off the dust of your feet."[44] "And whosoever shall not receive you, nor hear you, when ye depart thence, shake off the dust under your feet for a testimony against them. Verily I say unto you, It shall be more tolerable for Sodom and Gomorrha in the day of judgment, than for that city."[45] "And whosoever will not receive you, when ye go out of that city, shake off the very dust from your feet for a testimony against them."[46] "And in whatsoever place ye shall enter, and they receive you not in my name, ye shall leave a cursing instead of a blessing, by casting off the dust of your feet against them as a testimony, and cleansing your feet by the wayside."[47] "And in whatsoever house ye enter, and they receive you not, ye shall depart speedily from that house, and shake off the dust of your feet as a testimony against them."[48]

This ordinance is very serious and should not be performed without contacting your mission president. Elder James E. Talmage said this concerning this ordinance.

"Shaking the Dust from the Feet. — To ceremoniously shake the dust from one's feet as a testimony against another was understood by the Jews to symbolize a cessation of fellowship and a renunciation of all responsibility for consequences that might follow. It became an ordinance of accusation and testimony by the Lord's instructions to His apostles as cited in the text. In the current dispensation, the Lord has similarly directed His authorized servants to so testify against those who willfully and maliciously oppose the truth when authoritatively presented (see D&C 24:15; 60:15; 75:20; 84:92; 99:4). The responsibility of testifying before the Lord by this accusing symbol is so great that the means may be employed only under unusual and extreme conditions, as the Spirit of the Lord may direct." [49]

# Priesthood Ordinances: Conclusion

It is fairly easy to see that for the most part we need to remember to start with a name (if one is available), state our authority, do what needs to be done as far as blessing or consecrating or dedicating, and do it in the name of Jesus Christ.

We must always remember that these ordinances are priesthood ordinances and can only be effective if we are worthy of the priesthood and its use. When we act in the priesthood we are to be acting as the Lord if He were in our situation.

In almost every ordinance that we have covered, the direction of the Spirit is very necessary. We must live our lives so that we can receive the revelation that is associated with the priesthood and its blessings.

May we be blessed with the ability to overcome the world and enjoy the blessings of utilizing the priesthood to bless the lives of others.

Now for your assignment. Look for opportunities to exercise your priesthood as often as you possibly can. Remember that as an Elder you can perform all of the ordinances that anyone in the Aaronic Priesthood can. Pass the sacrament, prepare it and bless it, etc. If there is an opportunity to baptize someone, ordain someone, or utilize your priesthood power in any way, do it!

# Priesthood Ordinances: End Notes

[1]Bruce R. McConkie, Mormon Doctrine, pp. 548-549.

[2]Bruce R. McConkie, Mormon Doctrine, p. 91.

[3]Melchizedek Priesthood Personal Study Guide, 1985, p. 279.

[4]D&C 20:38-46.

[5]Melchizedek Priesthood Personal Study Guide, 1985, p. 280.

[6]Genesis 24:2.

[7]Ibid 48:13-19.

[8]Exodus 15:6.

[9]Joseph Fielding Smith, Answers to Gospel Questions, Volume 1, p. 158.

[10]Melchizedek Priesthood Handbook, 1984, p. 27.

[11]Ibid.

[12]Melchizedek Priesthood Personal Study Guide, 1985, p. 280.

[13]Ibid.

[14]Ibid.

[15]D&C 20:47-51.

[16]D&C 20:38-84.

[17]Joseph Fielding Smith, Doctrines of Salvation, Volume 3, p.155.

[18]Bruce R. McConkie, Mormon Doctrine, p. 549.

[19]Improvement Era, Volume 4, p. 230, January, 1901.

[20]Melchizedek Priesthood Personal Study Guide, 1985, p. 281.

[21]See Jacob 5; D&C 101; Revelation 11:4; Zachariah 4:11-14; Leviticus 8:6-12; and Exodus 27:20-21. Joseph Smith referred to the 88th section of the D&C as the Olive leaf.

[22]Joseph Fielding Smith, Answers to Gospel Questions, Volume 1, p. 153.

[23]Melchizedek Priesthood Personal Study Guide, 1985, p. 281.

[24]Ibid.

[25]Joseph F. Smith; Improvement Era, Volume 10, p. 308. Teachings of the Prophet Joseph Smith, pp. 224-225.

[26]Joseph Fielding Smith, Answers to Gospel Questions, Volume 1, p. 148.

[27]Ibid

[28]Melchizedek Priesthood Personal Study Guide, 1985, p. 281-282.

[29]Melchizedek Priesthood Personal Study Guide, 1985, p. 282.

[30]Bruce R. McConkie, Mormon Doctrine, p. 549.

[31]Melchizedek Priesthood Personal Study Guide, 1985, p. 282.

[32]Ibid.

[33]Joseph Fielding Smith, Doctrines of Salvation, Volume 3, pp. 169-172.

[34]Ibid.

[35]Melchizedek Priesthood Personal Study Guide, 1985, p. 283.

[36]Ibid.

[37]Ibid.

[38]Ibid.

[39]Ibid.

[40]Ibid.

[41]Melchizedek Priesthood Handbook, 1984, p. 29.

[42]Ibid.

[43]Ibid.


[44] Matt 10:14

[45] Mark 6: 11

[46] Luke 9:5

[47] D&C 24:15

[48] D&C 75:20

[49] Jesus the Christ, Ch.21, p.345

# CHAPTER 7

# I'M SO PROUD OF YOU!

I want you to take a minute and list all of your accomplishments. Go ahead, do it. Get out a piece of paper and a pen and write. Don't continue reading until you have written at least five things that you have accomplished that you are proud of. Don't just think about them. Stop right now and write them down. Have you got some good ones? Look over the list.

Now, I want you to put a check mark by each item on the list that did not require God's help. These should only be the items that you have accomplished without Him. Really think about it. Is there anything that we can do without Him? Can we breathe, walk, talk or even exist?

Should we be "proud" of our accomplishments or grateful to God? Obviously God makes all things possible. We should feel a humble reverence just to be able to live each day. Not a single item on your list should have a mark by it.

Pride is one of the most, if not the most, destructive things you can take into the mission field. If you feel that you are able to do the Lord's work without the help of the Lord, you will quickly find out that you are trying to do the impossible. "O Lord, I have trusted in thee, and I will trust in thee forever. I will not put my trust in the arm of flesh; for I know that cursed is he that putteth his trust in the arm of flesh. Yea, cursed is he that putteth his trust in man or maketh flesh his arm" (2 Nep 4:34).

As you read the scriptures you will find a recurring theme especially in the Book of Mormon. The people humble themselves and the Lord blesses them. Then they become proud of the blessings they have so the Lord causes them to be humble.

This 'pride cycle' repeats throughout the Book of Mormon. Wouldn't it be great if we could be blessed and humble at the same time? We would have continual prosperity. The closest the people of the Book of Mormon came to this state seems to be after the Lord appeared to the people as recorded in Fourth Nephi.

"AND it came to pass that the thirty and fourth year passed away, and also the thirty and fifth, and behold the disciples of Jesus had formed a church of Christ in all the lands round about. And as many as did come unto them, and did truly repent of their sins, were baptized in the name of Jesus; and they did also receive the Holy Ghost. And it came to pass in the thirty and sixth year, the people were all converted unto the Lord, upon all the face of the land, both Nephites and Lamanites, and there were no contentions and disputations among them, and every man did deal justly one with another. And they had all things common among them; therefore there were not rich and poor, bond and free, but they were all made free, and partakers of the heavenly gift. And it came to pass that the thirty and seventh year passed away also, and there still continued to be peace in the land. And there were great and marvelous works wrought by the disciples of Jesus, insomuch that they did heal the sick, and raise the dead, and cause the lame to walk, and the blind to receive their sight, and the deaf to hear; and all manner of miracles did they work among the children of men; and in nothing did they work miracles save it were in the name of Jesus. And thus did the thirty and eighth year pass away, and also the thirty and ninth, and forty and first, and the forty and second, yea, even until forty and nine years had passed away, and also the fifty and first, and the fifty and second; yea, and even until fifty and nine years had passed away. And the Lord did prosper them exceedingly in the land; yea, insomuch that they did build cities again where there had been cities burned. Yea, even that great city Zarahemla did they cause to be built again. But there were many cities which had been sunk, and waters came up in the stead thereof; therefore these cities could not be renewed. And now, behold, it came to pass that the people of Nephi did wax strong, and did multiply exceedingly fast, and became an exceedingly fair and delight-some people. And they were married, and given in marriage, and were blessed according to the multitude of the promises which the Lord had made unto them. And they did not walk any more after the performances and ordinances of the law of Moses; but they did walk after the commandments which they had received from their Lord and their God, continuing in fasting and prayer, and in meeting together oft both to pray and to hear the word of the Lord. And it came to pass that there was no contention among all the people, in all the land; but there were mighty miracles wrought among the disciples of Jesus. And it came to pass that the seventy and first year passed away, and also the seventy and second year, yea, and in fine, till the seventy and ninth year had passed away; yea, even an hundred years had passed away, and the disciples of Jesus, whom he had chosen, had all gone to the paradise of God, save it were the three who should tarry; and there were other disciples ordained in their stead; and also many of that generation had passed away. And it came to pass that there was no contention in the land, because of the love of God which did dwell in the hearts of the people. And there were no envyings, nor strifes, nor tumults, nor whoredoms, nor lyings, nor murders, nor any manner of lasciviousness; and surely there could not be a happier people among all the people who had been created by the hand of God. There were no robbers, nor murderers, neither were there Lamanites, nor any manner of -ites; but they were in one, the children of Christ, and heirs to the kingdom of God. And how blessed were they! For the Lord did bless them in all their doings; yea, even they were blessed and prospered until an hundred and ten years had passed away; and the first generation from Christ had passed away, and there was no contention in all the land. And it came to pass that Nephi, he that kept this last record, (and he kept it upon the plates of Nephi) died, and his son Amos kept it in his stead; and he kept it upon the plates of Nephi also. And he kept it eighty and four years, and there was still peace in the land, save it were a small part of the people who had revolted from the church and taken upon them the name of Lamanites; therefore there began to be Lamanites again in the land. And it came to pass that Amos died also, (and it was an hundred and ninety and four years from the coming of Christ) and his son Amos kept the record in his stead; and he also kept it upon the plates of Nephi; and it was also written in the book of Nephi, which is this book. And it came to pass that two hundred years had passed away; and the second generation had all passed away save it were a few. And now I, Mormon, would that ye should know that the people had multiplied, insomuch that they were spread upon all the face of the land, and that they had become exceedingly rich, because of their prosperity in Christ. And now, in this two hundred and first year there began to be among them those who were lifted up in *pride*, such as the wearing of costly apparel, and all manner of fine pearls, and of the fine things of the world. And from that time forth they did have their goods and their substance no more common among them. And they began to be divided into classes; and they began to build up churches unto themselves to get gain, and began to deny the true church of Christ. And it came to pass that when two hundred and ten years had passed away there were many churches in the land; yea, there were many churches which professed to know the Christ, and yet they did deny the more parts of his gospel, insomuch that they did receive all manner of wickedness, and did administer that which was sacred unto him to whom it had been forbidden because of unworthiness. And this church did multiply exceedingly because of iniquity, and because of the power of Satan who did get hold upon their hearts" (4 Nephi 1-28, italics added).

These people were pleased to have everything in common and to make sure that everyone was taken care of and in need of nothing. They magnified their priesthood and there were many healings. The people genuinely loved one another. Then, after 200 years, pride crept into some of their hearts and they began to slide down the path that led to bloodshed and war.

Harold B. Lee said that humility is a rare virtue—once you

become humble you become proud that you're humble. If we can learn to remain humble by reminding ourselves who we are in the grand scheme of things and that Father is the only one who literally knows everything, maybe we can keep our hearts free from pride.

Even before the beginning of time, pride caused a huge problem—the largest problem that we have ever witnessed, even though we no longer remember the incident. It happened in the preexistence. Heavenly Father had a plan. It was the unchangeable plan of salvation. He presented it to us, His children. Jehovah stepped forward and said that He would be willing to participate in the plan just as it had been outlined. Lucifer had a different idea. He said that he would change the plan because he had a better way to do it. He would force everyone back into God's presence. On the surface, it might sound like his real motivation was a love for his brothers and sisters and he only wanted to insure that we would all return to God and become like our Father. However, there is one sentence that tells us the real reason that he set forth this new idea.

"Behold, here am I, send me, I will be thy son, and I will redeem all mankind, that one soul shall not be lost, and surely I will do it; wherefore *give me thine honor*" (Moses 4:1, italics added).

Lucifer wanted the glory and honor of the Father. That was his reason for wanting everyone to return to the Celestial Kingdom. He wanted to have the honor. What pride and arrogance! He thought he could change the plan of salvation, that he knew better than the Father what should be done and because he knew better he felt that he deserved the honor of God!

Because of that pride, one third of the hosts of Heaven were

99

eventually lost forever!

Now let's look at the response of Jehovah.

"But, behold, my Beloved Son, which was my Beloved and Chosen from the beginning, said unto me—*Father, thy will be done, and the glory be thine forever*" (Moses 4:2, italics added).

Note the vast difference in the two responses. He who was so full of pride was cast out forever and He who demonstrated humility became the Savior of the world.

Now I want you to think for a minute about the last time that your parents or a priesthood leader asked you to do something. How did you respond? Did you feel great humility and were you submissive, or did prideful thoughts run through your mind?

I really don't think that it would have been a major problem in that grand council in heaven if Lucifer had simply said something like, "Father, what if we made it so everyone was forced to come back, would that be a good idea?" Father probably would have lovingly explained again about the laws of free agency and how it was essential to prove ourselves, so force would not be acceptable. Then if Lucifer had simply said, "OK, I was just wondering," it would not have erupted into what happened. (Of course, we realize that without the fall of Lucifer, the plan would have been thwarted.)

In our earthly existence, pride seems to come from at least two sources. First, we genuinely feel that we are better than someone else, that we know more or we can do more or we are smarter, etc. This may all be true, but if we lose the realization that we are all of those things because of blessings from a loving God and we feel that we have gained those advantages all by ourselves, we lose our humility and we become so full of ourselves that we don't listen to others. Second, we fear men more than God. Peer pressure can unveil pride in our lives. If a young girl wants to wear immodest clothing because that's what is socially acceptable, even though she knows it is not what the Lord would want her to wear, she fears her peers more than she fears God. If she wears the immodest clothing, she stands in defiance of God. She is in essence telling Him what Lucifer told Him—I know better than you so I will do what I want to, so there!

Sometimes it is extremely difficult to break the bands of pride. If you tell someone who is proud that they are proud, you usually find that they are too proud to admit it. Sometimes it takes an act of God to humble them. Of course you will remember what happened to Saul (who later was called Paul) in the New Testament. He was persecuting the Christians but, like Alma in the book of Mormon, he was visited by a heavenly being and driven from his great pride to humility (See Acts 9). I always ask Father to help me to remain humble enough to avoid being "knocked to my knees."

When we admit our weaknesses in true humility, we offer fertile ground to the Lord to perform His great life-changing work on us. Life is too short for us to waste time trying to convince others that we know absolutely everything there is to know. We need to spend as much time as we can learning how to improve and then do the work necessary to change our lives for the better. If we do that, we will find ourselves eternally in the presence of our Creator. If we are convinced that we don't need to change, so we just continue to amble on, we may find ourselves lost. "Beware of pride, lest ye become as the Nephites of old"(D&C 38:39). "Behold, the pride of this nation, or the people of the Nephites,hath proven their destruction" (Moroni 8:27).

Here are a couple more examples of the devastating effects of pride. The first is that of Laman and Lemuel, the sons of Lehi. If you read my other book *Dare to Prepare* you will remember that I think that Laman and Lemuel did some pretty brave things in the beginning of their journey in the wilderness. What they did not do, however, was to soften their hearts like Nephi, for after he prayed, he was given further light and knowledge.

"And it came to pass that I beheld my brethren, and they were disputing one with another concerning the things which my father had spoken unto them. For he truly spake many great things unto them, which were hard to be understood, save a man should inquire of the Lord; and *they being hard in their hearts, therefore they did not look unto the Lord as they ought*" (1 Nephi 15:2-3, italics added).

Their hearts were hard and they thought they knew everything, so why go to God and ask Him for anything? After all, what could He tell them? Eventually, this lack of humility caused two great nations to war until literally millions had been wiped off the face of the earth.

Another great example is the account of the serpent that Moses raised on a staff for the children of Israel. You may recall that the Israelites were complaining about being in the wilderness and they were even complaining about the food that the Lord was providing them. Their hearts were so hardened that the Lord caused fiery serpents to go among the people and many were bit by the serpents and died. Finally, the survivors came to Moses and repented of their pride and the hardness of their hearts and asked Moses to do something to save them. Moses prayed and the Lord told him to make a brass serpent and put it on a pole and raise it among the people. All who had been bitten and were willing to look at the brass serpent would be healed (See Num. 21: 8-9). In the Book of Mormon we receive more information about the incident. We find that there were those who were so hard in their hearts that they would not even do the simple task of looking at the serpent on the pole!

"Behold, he was spoken of by Moses; yea, and behold a type was raised up in the wilderness, that whosoever would look upon it might live. And many did look and live. But few understood the meaning of those things, and this because of the hardness of their hearts. But there were many who were so hardened that they would not look, therefore they perished. Now the reason they would not look is because they did not believe that it would heal them. O my brethren, if ye could be healed by merely casting about your eyes that ye might be healed, would ye not behold quickly, or would ye rather harden your hearts in unbelief, and be slothful, that ye would not cast about your eyes, that ye might perish?" (Alma 33:19-21).

Pride cost those who had been bitten and who would not look upon the serpent to lose their lives. The Lord shows us the way and we need to improve daily in humility. We must accept that we are not perfect and we need Him to help us change. He will help us if we are willing to simply look!

The last example I will relate is one of the parables of James E. Talmage. It is called "The Parable of the Unwise Bee." I would rather that you read it in his powerful words.

## The Parable of the Unwise Bee

Sometimes I find myself under obligations of work requiring quiet and seclusion such as neither my comfortable office nor the cozy study at home insures. My favorite retreat is an upper room in the tower of a large building, well removed from the noise and confusion of the city streets. The room is somewhat difficult to access and relatively secure against human intrusion. Therein I have spent many peaceful and busy hours with books and pen.

I am not always without visitors, however, especially in summertime; for when I sit with windows open, flying insects occasionally find entrance and share the place with me. These self-invited guests are not unwelcome. Many a time I have laid down the pen and, forgetful of my theme, have watched with interest the activities of these winged visitants, with an after-thought that the time so spent had not been wasted, for is it not true that even a butterfly, a beetle, or a bee may be a bearer of lessons to the receptive student?

A wild bee from the neighboring hills once flew into the room, and at intervals during an hour or more I caught the pleasing hum of its flight. The little creature realized that it was a prisoner, yet all its efforts to find the exit through the partly opened casement failed. When ready to close up the room and leave, I threw the window wide and tried at first to guide and then to drive the bee to liberty and safety, knowing well that if left in the room it would die as other insects there entrapped had perished in the dry atmosphere of the enclosure. The more I tried to drive it out, the more determinedly did it oppose and resist my efforts. Its erstwhile peaceful hum developed into an angry roar; its darting flight became hostile and threatening.

Then it caught me off my guard and stung my hand—the hand that would have guided it to freedom. At last it alighted on a pendant attached to the ceiling, beyond my reach of help or injury. The sharp pain of its unkind sting aroused in me rather pity than anger. I knew the inevitable penalty of its mistaken opposition and defiance, and I had to leave the crea-ture to its fate. Three days later I returned to the room and found the dried, lifeless body of the bee on the writing table. It had paid for its stubbornness with its life.

To the bee's shortsightedness and selfish misunder-standing I was a foe, a persistent persecutor, a mortal enemy bent on its destruction; while in truth I was its friend, offering it ransom of the life it had put in forfeit through its own error, striving to redeem it, in spite of itself, from the prison house of death and restore it to the outer air of liberty.

Are we so much wiser than the bee that no analogy lies between its unwise course and our lives? We are prone to contend, sometimes with vehemence and anger, against the adversity which after all may be the manifestation of superior wisdom and loving care, directed against our temporary comfort for our permanent blessing. In the tribulations and sufferings of mortality there is a divine ministry which only the godless soul can wholly fail to discern. To many the loss of wealth has been a boon, a providential means of leading or driving them from the confines of selfish indulgence to the sunshine and the open, where boundless opportunity waits on effort. Disappointment, sorrow, and affliction may be the expression of an all-wise Father's kindness.

Consider the lesson of the unwise bee!

"Trust in the Lord with all thine heart; and lean not unto thine own understanding. In all thy ways acknowledge him, and he shall direct thy paths" ( Prov. 3:5-6 ). (James E. Talmage)

Shake off your pride on your own before the Lord finds the need to drive you to your knees. Always seek the council of your leaders and parents and then have the ability to say they are right and do something about it.

Remember the great example of humility that the Lord gave us when he took the time to tenderly wash the feet of the apostles. He showed that to be the best servant one must demonstrate humility (See John 13).

Now for your assignment. I hope you are not too proud to

do it! In sincerity, ask someone to whom you are very close to tell you at least one thing (but no more than two) that they feel you could improve upon. I don't mean things like your tennis game, but things more of a spiritual nature, like listening to what your parents or priesthood leaders have to say with a truly open heart, in humility, and with a teachable soul. When they have given you an idea or two, take it to the Lord and confirm with Him that this is something you should work on. Then, really work on it! Realize that you are not perfect and that you do need to learn and progress. Get rid of the pride and make a real effort to change a part of your life in humility.

Also, during the coming week, I want you to try to catch yourself when pride arises. Maybe your friend will be talking to you and you will be thinking you have a better story or you can do something better than your friend. Whatever the source, I want you to catch yourself showing pride and then think how you might have better handled the situation. When you have found something to work on and are working on it, go on to the next chapter.

# CHAPTER 8

# WHICH CHURCH IS RIGHT?

Do you have friends who are of another faith? Do you know people who believe in Jesus Christ but don't really have a "religion"? How important would it be to know if there was only one that was true—totally true, and which religion it was? The prophet Joseph Smith showed by example that it was important enough to at least pray about with real intent. "My object in going to inquire of the Lord was to know which of all the sects was right, that I might know which to join. No sooner, therefore, did I get possession of myself, so as to be able to speak, than I asked the Personages who stood above me in the light, which of all the sects was right" (JSH 1:18).

Let's explore some things that will hopefully bolster your testimony and help you determine if The Church of Jesus Christ of Latter-day Saints is the only true and living church on the face of the earth.

Much of what we discuss here will be taken from three sources. The first is an old discussion that missionaries used to use called the Scroll Discussion. The second is The Baptismal Discussion that we used in my mission field and the third is a church pamphlet entitled Which Church is Right? written by Elder Mark E. Peterson of the Quorum of the Twelve Apostles.

This chapter will mostly contain information without stories or activities, but the doctrine herein is extremely powerful. This information is designed to help you with your own testimony and knowledge. These discussions are no longer used that I am aware of. One of the reasons that they are not used is because they basically prove the Church to be true. We are not about proving; we are about setting an environment wherein the Holy Ghost can testify of the truthfulness of the gospel. Then, a testimony from the Spirit results instead of just a testimony of knowledge. Those who receive a testimony from a member of the Godhead are much less likely to become inactive or turn away from what they have felt.

With that said, let's explore some of the things that help us to understand the truthfulness of the Church.

From the beginning of time on this earth, God has communed with man. The men He has called to receive His word are called prophets. Prophets are, almost by definition, those who speak with God, as did Adam, Noah, Abraham, Moses and others. It makes sense in our troubled world that we could use the help of prophets today. Certainly we believe that God loves His children as much today as He did in times past. There has never been a time on the earth when we have needed His help more than now. If God loves us and if He can communicate with us, it stands to reason that He would call prophets today just as He did in times of old so that He can communicate with us. There is no reason that He would not want to speak to us today unless He felt that we did not need Him.

God has not left us alone. He has given us prophets. From Joseph Smith to the current day we have had a prophet on the earth.

In the meridian of time, the Savior Jesus Christ organized His church. Of course we believe that Jesus Christ was perfect. So ask yourself these questions. Can someone who is perfect organize something that is not perfect? If something is perfect, does it change? If you answered no to both questions then it stands to reason that the organization of the church at the time of Christ was perfect. He organized it with twelve living apostles. He himself was the mouthpiece of God and as such fulfilled the role of a prophet. If He organized it perfectly and perfect things do not change, then if the church of Jesus Christ is on the earth it should be organized in the same way, with a living prophet and twelve apostles. Most churches are eliminated by this simple fact. The Church of Jesus Christ of Latter-day Saints does have a living prophet and twelve apostles.

Is there evidence of a need to keep at twelve the number of the apostles? Yes, it is shown by the fact that when Judas killed himself after betraying the Savior, his position in the Quorum of the Twelve Apostles was filled by Matthias.

"Wherefore of these men which have companied with us all the time that the Lord Jesus went in and out among us, beginning from the baptism of John, unto that same day that he was taken up from us, must one be ordained to be a witness with us of his resurrection. And they appointed two, Joseph called Barsabas, who was surnamed Justus, and Matthias. And they prayed, and said, Thou, Lord, which knowest the hearts of all men, shew whether of these two thou hast chosen, That he may take part of this ministry and apostleship, from which Judas by transgression fell, that he might go to his own place. And they gave forth their lots; and the lot fell upon Matthias; and he was numbered with the eleven apostles (Acts 1:21-26).

Acts 13:1-3 and 14:14 record the calling of both Saul and Barnabas to the apostleship to fill other vacancies. It is obvious that they were maintaining the number of twelve that was set up by a perfect Being.

Other evidence of the true and living church is found in an often misinterpreted passage of scripture found in Matthew.

"When Jesus came into the coasts of Caesarea Philippi, he asked his disciples, saying, Whom do men say that I the Son of man am? And they said, Some say that thou art John the Baptist: some, Elias; and others, Jeremias, or one of the prophets. He saith unto them, But whom say ye that I am? And Simon Peter answered and said, Thou art the Christ, the Son of the living God. And Jesus answered and said unto him, Blessed art thou, Simon Bar-jona: for flesh and blood hath not revealed it unto thee, but my Father which is in heaven. And I say also unto thee, That thou art Peter, and upon this rock I will build my church; and the gates of hell shall not prevail against it" (Matt 16:13-18).

Many quote only the last verse and claim that the Lord was telling Peter that he would be the leader of the church. When taken in full context, it is clear to see that the Lord was referring to revelation as being the "rock" upon which his church would be built. Thus, continuing revelation from God is another witness to the kingdom of God. We claim to have the Holy Ghost and continuing revelation.

Now you may wonder about the time between the Savior's earthly existence and the time of Joseph Smith. Didn't God love those people as much as He loved those before that time and as much as He loves us? Of course He did! His removal of the gospel from the earth during the "dark ages" shows that love. Just as He showed his love for His children during the time of the flood of Noah's day.

Those who lived in Noah's day had become so wicked that there was no way to turn them away from the wicked things they were doing. If there were to be children born into this state of wickedness, they would not have had a chance to live the gospel and those who were already on the earth were simply damning themselves further every day of their existence. A loving Father cleansed the earth for the sakes of those who had inhabited it and those who would be born to them.

The same idea is true at the time of the apostasy. After the Lord had been crucified, the Apostles were separated and killed. The parable of the Husbandman refers to these events:

"Hear another parable: There was a certain householder, which planted a vineyard, and hedged it round about, and digged a winepress in it, and built a tower, and let it out to husbandmen, and went into a far country: And when the time of the fruit drew near, he sent his servants to the husbandmen, that they might receive the fruits of it. And the husbandmen took his servants , and beat one, and killed another, and stoned another. Again, he sent other servants more than the first: and they did unto them likewise. But last of all he sent unto them his son, saying, They will reverence my son. But when the husbandmen saw the son, they said among themselves, This is the heir; come, let us kill him, and let us seize on his inheritance. And they caught him, and cast him out of the vineyard, and slew him. When the lord therefore of the vineyard cometh, what will he do unto those husbandmen? They say unto him, He will miserably destroy those wicked men, and will let out his vineyard unto other husbandmen, which shall render him the fruits in their seasons" (Matt 21:33-41).

Father had sent His servants the prophets to the people and they were rejected and killed so He sent His son who was also killed. As a result of this treatment, Father removed the gospel from the earth so it would not be desecrated further. This time of apostasy with a restoration to come were testified of in the scriptures.

Speaking of the earth just prior to the last days, the prophet Isaiah said, "For, behold, the darkness shall cover the earth, and gross darkness the people" (Isaiah 60:2). Amos said, "Behold, the days come, saith the Lord GOD, that I will send a famine in the land, not a famine of bread, nor a thirst for water, but of hearing the words of the LORD And they shall wander from sea to sea, and from the north even to the east, they shall run to and fro to seek the word of the LORD, and shall not find it" (Amos 8:11-12). When the apostle Paul wrote to the

Thesselonians about the second coming of the Savior he said, "Let no man deceive you by any means: for that day shall not come, except there come a falling away first, and that man of sin be revealed, the son of perdition" (2 Thes. 2:3). If you want to find more scriptures about the apostasy, just look in the topical guide. There are dozens of them.

Here, in a nutshell, is basically what happened after the death of the Savior. Christ had commanded His apostles to go out into the world and preach the word to everyone (See Mark 16:15). They followed that command and began traveling to preach. When they baptized a group of people they ordained either a presiding elder or a bishop over the group depending on its size. Bishops were over the larger groups. They would then move on in order to continue to fulfill their calling to travel and preach. The Apostles continued to be the general authorities and the presiding elders and bishops were local authorities. Titus, Timothy and Linus are examples of these local leaders. They all had the same authority.

The Apostles tried to keep in touch with the local leaders through letters, several of which are in the New Testament. As you read the letters written by Paul, James, Peter and others, you will understand that they were constantly trying to keep the church from apostasy.

Persecution was severe, first from the Jews and then from the Romans. Many members of the church were killed. The Apostles, who were out in different areas preaching began to be killed and they could not reunite in order to reorganize themselves into a quorum of twelve.

Andrew was crucified at Patras (Greece) in A.D. 60. He suffered on the cross for two days, while preaching and encouraging the people gathered around him.

Bartholomew died in Albanopolis, Armenia, where he was beaten, then flayed alive, afterwards crucified and lastly beheaded.

There are two views concerning the death of James, the Son of Alphaeus. According to the first view, the Jews beat and stoned him to death at the age of ninety-four, finally dashing out his brains with a fuller's club. The second version says that he was crucified in Persia.

James the Son of Zebedee was beheaded.

John was thrown into a boiling caldron of oil and miraculously survived, after which he was banished to the Island of Patmos.

Judas (Not Iscariot) was killed by magicians with clubs and stones in Persia; according to another version he was crucified in Edessa, Turkey, in A.D. 72.

Matthew was martyred with a spear in the city of Nadabah, Ethiopia, in A.D. 60.

Philip is believed to have been martyred in Hierapolis.

Peter was crucified head downwards at his request.

Simon Zelotes was crucified in Britain in A.D. 74.

Thomas was martyred with a spear in India.

Matthias was stoned to death and then beheaded by the Jews in Jerusalem.

During this time of great tumult, the Quorum of the Twelve dwindled to eleven, then ten, and so on, until there was only one left—John the Beloved, who had been promised immortality (See John 21:22-23). It is interesting to note that John, while on the isle of Patmos, had outlived both Peter and Paul and would have been the leader of the church.

The church was in serious trouble. The events of the apostasy which the Apostles had written about in their letters were coming to pass. The persecution became more intense as the government got into the act under the direction of Nero in the first century A.D. Strange doctrines began to enter the church because there were no general authorities to correct them.

Some examples would be the adoration of the mother of Jesus, the baptism of children, and the rituals that became the Mass.

The various local branches of the church began to practice different doctrines and arguments ensued. Those who lead larger congregations claimed to have more authority than those with a smaller following. Branches began to adopt doctrines that were popular with the government in order to slow persecution and increase their membership.

Constantine, who was a sun worshipper, saw political advantage in nurturing the Christians. He made Christianity the state religion so that he could have a huge influence over it. He called a gathering of the bishops and basically outlined what the beliefs would be. Those who did not conform were either convinced to do so or killed. Constantine appointed new bishops to fill the vacancies he had created, even though he had no religious authority to do this. Although he had committed murder in his own family, Constantine gathered together the Nicene council which lead to the creation of the Nicene Creed which incorrectly defines the nature of God.

The succeeding emperors continued to rule over the church. The members could have no say in political matters other than to ratify what the emperor was doing.

Quarreling about the power of the bishops eventually narrowed to two bishops—one in Rome and the other in Constantinople. They both excommunicated each other and formed their own congregations.

Martin Luther spoke out against the selling of indulgences and he was excommunicated. Luther believed in salvation by grace alone. Prince John of Saxony believed what Luther said and set up the Lutheran Church. The kings in Scandinavia set up the Protestant faith.

About this time, King Henry the Eighth decided he wanted to divorce his wife. When Rome denied him a divorce, he took church property and set up the Church of England.

At this point, all of the churches were state organizations and had no direct authority from God. The apostasy was complete and the true and living gospel was nowhere to be found.

It only stands to reason that if there was going to be an apostasy, there would have to be a restoration before the return of the Lord in glory and power. That restoration was brought forth through the prophet Joseph Smith. Now, as a missionary, you already know the story of Joseph Smith very well so I won't go into it here. When he was on the earth, all of the pure doctrines of the Lord had been changed, and/or directed by the state by people without authority to do so. If the right church had been upon the earth when Joseph Smith prayed and asked God which one it was, don't you think that God would have told him and asked him to join it? Of course He would, but the true church no longer existed upon the earth.

As we discussed earlier, prophets are men who speak with and in behalf of God. We know that Joseph Smith spoke with God in the sacred grove, so by definition, Joseph Smith is a prophet.

A few years after the appearance of the Father and the Son to Joseph, he was visited by the angel Moroni and was ultimately given the plates which he translated into what we call The Book of Mormon. Let's spend a little time right now and look to the Bible to help us in understanding the origin of the Book of Mormon.

Adam lived approximately 4,000 B.C. He was the father of the entire human race. We did not evolve from monkeys or come from some primeval sludge. We were created in the image of God! Seth, the son of Adam, carried the familial line on to Enoch and from there it extended to Noah, who lived about 2,400 to 2,300 B.C. Noah had three sons; Ham (who, although forbidden, married Egyptus) whose descendants were black; Shem, who was the father of the covenant people; and

Japeth, who was the father of people of Latins and Oriental descent (see bible dictionary).

Through Shem's line came Abram, who was later called Abraham, which means father of many nations. He lived roughly 2,000 to 1,900 B.C. God called Abram out of the land of Ur and into the land of Canaan. God wanted to make a covenant with Abraham. In order to test and strengthen Abraham, God commanded him to sacrifice his son Isaac (see Gen. 22).

In Genesis 17:1-8, God and Abraham make a covenant, the Abrahamic Covenant. Abraham makes one promise, to be perfect, and God makes four promises:

1. Abraham will be the father of many nations. He will have many descendants.

2. Kings shall come from the loins of Abraham. Saul, David Solomon and the King of Kings, even Jesus Christ, came from the loins of Abraham.

3. He was promised the land of Canaan, the promised land.

4. God said that He would be a God to Abraham and his seed. Abraham and his seed would have the teachings of God.

IT IS VERY IMPORTANT TO REMEMBER THE FOUR BLESSINGS OF THE ABRAHAMIC COVENANT.

Abraham had two sons; Ishmael (the father of the Arabic people) and Isaac, with whom the covenant was again established in Genesis 17:19-21. Isaac's descendants have the teachings of God because it was promised to Abraham that they would. Isaac had two sons, Esau, who, although he was born first, gave up his birthright for a mess of pottage (See Gen. 25:29-34), and Jacob. God changed Jacob's name to Israel and reestablished the covenant once again (see Gen. 35:10-12). Israel's descendants would dwell in Canaan and have the teachings of God as per the covenant.

Now it starts to get a little bit confusing as we try to follow Jacob's descendants because. He had twelve sons born to two wives and two concubines. Jacob (Israel) served Laban for seven years to gain the hand of Rachel and instead Laban gave him Leah, who was the oldest sister. Israel had to agree to serve Laban for another seven years in order to have Rachel for a wife, which he did. Leah was given a maid named Zilpath and Rachel was given a maid named Bilhah. The children were born in this order . . . Reuben (Leah), Simeon (Leah), Levi (Leah), Judah (Leah), Dan (Bilhah), Naphtali (Bilhah), Gad (Zilpath), Asher (Zilpath), Issachar (Leah), Zebulum (Leah), Joseph (Rachel) and Benjamin (Rachel) (See Gen. 35). They all had the teachings of God because it was part of the covenant.

Joseph is sold into Egypt by his brothers and becomes their savior during the famine. The family is finally reunited. It is a long but wonderful story(See Gen. 37-48).

In Genesis 49, Israel gathers his sons together to give them his final blessing because he knows he is going to die. In verses 8-10, Judah is promised that Christ will come through his loins.

What we want to focus on is Joseph's blessing. It is found in verses 22-26 of Genesis 49. Joseph is told he will be a fruitful bough (many descendants), by a well (signifies water), with branches that run over a wall (a wall is a barrier, the greatest barrier to these people was the ocean), his branches (descendants) would cross over the wall (ocean). We are told that the archers sorely grieved him. This refers to his brothers' disdain for him. He was made strong which was demonstrated by his gift of interpretation of dreams and his high position in Egypt. He was promised blessings of the breast and womb (he would be fruitful and have descendants).

In verse 26 Israel tells Joseph that the blessing he is receiving from his father is a greater blessing than his progenitors (forefathers) received. As the most favored son, Joseph was receiving the greatest blessing. A blessing even greater than Jacob's (Israel's) forefathers, Isaac and Abraham.

How could Joseph's blessing be any greater than the blessing given to Abraham? Abraham was promised that kings would come from his loins. Could Joseph have more kings come from his loins than Abraham did? It would be impossible because Joseph is a descendant of Abraham. Abraham was promised that he would have many descendants. Could Joseph have more descendants than Abraham? Once again, it would be impossible for the same reason cited above. Abraham was promised that his descendants would have the teachings of God. Could Joseph's descendants have more of the teachings of God than Abraham's? Once again, the answer is no. The only area wherein Abraham's blessing was limited was in the land he was promised. Abraham was given the land of Canaan for an inheritance. Could Joseph receive more land than Abraham? The answer is yes! Not only could he receive more land, but this is the only area of the blessing of Abraham in which Joseph's blessing could be greater.

Where is this land that would increase Joseph's blessing to be greater than Abraham's? According to verse 26 it says the "utmost bound of the everlasting hills." The dictionary defines 'utmost' as the greatest extremes or furthermost. This blessing was given to Joseph on the eastern hemisphere. The utmost bound of the eastern hemisphere is the western hemisphere. In the term "everlasting hills," everlasting means either something that will endure forever or something without beginning or end. In North America, rising out of the floor of the ocean, is a chain of mountains which forms the Aleutian Islands, the Canadian Rockies, the Rocky Mountains, the Sierra Madres and the Andes before it drops back into the ocean. This is one unbroken string of mountains.

Israel was talking about America being the land that Joseph's descendants would receive. This is where the blessing is greater than Abraham's! Moses, as well, suggests that Joseph's blessing is a blessing of land (See Deuteronomy 33:13).

Now let's talk about how Joseph's descendants got to America. A quick history review would be in order. Moses led the children of Israel to the promised land. Joshua took Israel into the promised land. The promised land was ruled by judges then kings (Saul, David, Solomon and Reheboam). At the time of Reheboam, ten-and-a-half tribes rebelled against his rule and went into the land northward and set up their own kingdom of Israel, ruled by Jeroboam.

This was about 975 B.C. Judah and half of the tribe of Benjamin stayed in the southern part of Canaan and called their kingdom Judah. About 721 B. C., ten-and-a-half tribes were led into captivity by the kings of Assyria. When they were released, they went northward and became the lost ten tribes. We know that they have the teachings of God because it was promised to Abraham.

In 600 B. C., Lehi, a descendant of Joseph who lived in the kingdom of Judah was told by the Lord to leave Jerusalem because the great city was going to be destroyed. Lehi and his family, along with Ishmael and his family, left Jerusalem and came to the Americas. Nebuchadnezzar, the king of Babylon, destroyed Jerusalem (See Jer. 46:13). Lehi's family would have the teachings of God because it was part of the promise.

In Ezekiel 37:15-22 we read:

15. The word of the LORD came again unto me, saying,
16. Moreover, thou son of man, take thee one stick, and write upon it, For Judah, and for the children of Israel his companions: then take another stick, and write upon it, For Joseph, the stick of Ephraim, and for all the house of Israel his companions:
17. And join them one to another into one stick; and they

shall become one in thine hand.

18. And when the children of thy people shall speak unto thee, saying, Wilt thou not shew us what thou meanest by these?

19. Say unto them, Thus saith the Lord GOD; Behold, I will take the stick of Joseph, which is in the hand of Ephraim, and the tribes of Israel his fellows, and will put them with him, even with the stick of Judah, and make them one stick, and they shall be one in mine hand.

20. And the sticks whereon thou writest shall be in thine hand before their eyes.

21. And say unto them, Thus saith the Lord GOD; Behold, I will take the children of Israel from among the heathen, whither they be gone, and will gather them on every side, and bring them into their own land:

22. And I will make them one nation in the land upon the mountains of Israel; and one king shall be king to them all: and they shall be no more two nations, neither shall they be divided into two kingdoms any more at all.

Verses 15-16 tell us that there are two sticks or records being kept. One is the stick of Judah which is the Bible. The other is the stick of Joseph, which would be the equivalent history of the descendants of Joseph, who we have already shown, are on the American continent. This stick is the Book of Mormon!

Is there any other book that claims to be joined together with the stick of Judah? There is none save the Book of Mormon.

Verses 20-21 tell us that after the two sticks have been joined together into one, the children of Israel would be gathered into their own land. On May 15, 1948, by an act of the United Nations, Israel was given back to the Jews. The gathering spoken of has commenced. This means that if there is a book that fulfills the prophecy of Ezekiel, it must have come forth prior to this date in 1948, prior to the beginning of the gathering of Israel. If a book came out now and claimed to be the stick of Joseph, it would be too late. The only book that claims to be the stick of Joseph and thus fulfills this prophecy is the Book of Mormon.

According to the Abrahamic covenant, Joseph and his descendants must have the teachings of God. Where? In America. Where are those teachings recorded? In the Book of Mormon!

Does it make any sense that God would only reveal His teachings to the people living around Jerusalem? In fact, He told those whom he loved in Jerusalem that He had to go and teach the gospel to His "other sheep." "And other sheep I have, which are not of this fold: them also I must bring, and they shall hear my voice; and there shall be one fold, and one shepherd" (John 10:16). He was speaking about the people in the Americas—Joseph's descendants (See 3 Nephi 15:21). He even stated to the people in the Americas that He still had others to visit (See 3 Nephi 16:1-3) that He might fulfill the covenant because they too had the promise of the teachings of God. This probably refers to the lost ten tribes.

The Book of Mormon is the record of the dealings of God with the prophets and people on the American continent. It fulfills all of the requirements of the stick of Joseph and the prophecies of Ezekiel.

Now let's look at another source of confirmation of the Book of Mormon from the Bible. Let's turn to Isaiah chapter 29. Verses 9-10 describe the "Dark Ages." He tells us that the prophets and seers have been covered.

In verse eleven, God tells us that the darkness will end with a vision. He never intended us to remain in darkness forever. "And the vision of all is become unto you as the words of a book that is sealed, which men deliver to one that is learned, saying, Read this, I pray thee: and he saith, I cannot; for it is sealed" (Isaiah 29:11). We needed prophets and seers to have visions to bring the gospel back (See Amos 3:7). How will we know the prophet? The vision will come forth in the form of a sealed book. You will recall that two-thirds of the Book of Mormon were sealed and were not translated. It is the sealed book!

It tells us that the words of the book, not the book itself, would be delivered to a learned man who would proclaim that he could not read a sealed book. I will here include a portion of the Pearl of Great Price from the history of Joseph Smith wherein he tells us what happened in the fulfilling of this scripture.

"By this timely aid was I enabled to reach the place of my destination in Pennsylvania; and immediately after my arrival there I commenced copying the characters off the plates. I copied a considerable number of them, and by means of the Urim and Thummim I translated some of them, which I did between the time I arrived at the house of my wife's father, in the month of December, and the February following. Sometime in this month of February, the aforementioned Mr. Martin Harris came to our place, got the characters which I had drawn off the plates, and started with them to the city of New York. For what took place relative to him and the characters, I refer to his own account of the circumstances, as he related them to me after his return, which was as follows: "I went to the city of New York, and presented the characters which had been translated, with the translation thereof, to Professor Charles Anthon, a gentleman celebrated for his literary attainments. Professor Anthon stated that the translation was correct, more so than any he had before seen translated from the Egyptian. I then showed him those which were not yet translated, and he said that they were Egyptian, Chaldaic, Assyriac, and Arabic;

and he said they were true characters. He gave me a certificate, certifying to the people of Palmyra that they were true characters, and that the translation of such of them as had been translated was also correct. I took the certificate and put it into my pocket, and was just leaving the house, when Mr. Anthon called me back, and asked me how the young man found out that there were gold plates in the place where he found them. I answered that an angel of God had revealed it unto him. He then said to me, 'Let me see that certificate.' I accordingly took it out of my pocket and gave it to him, when he took it and tore it to pieces, saying that there was no such thing now as ministering of angels, and that if I would bring the plates to him he would translate them. I informed him that part of the plates were sealed, and that I was forbidden to bring them. He replied, 'I cannot read a sealed book.' I left him and went to Dr. Mitchell, who sanctioned what Professor Anthon had said respecting both the characters and the translation."

Verses 12-14 of Isaiah 29 tell us that the Lord chose an unlearned man to bring forth the book which would bring to pass a "marvelous work among this people, even a marvelous work and a wonder" (See vs. 14).

## THE BOOK OF MORMON IS THAT MARVELOUS WORK AND WONDER!

In verse 17, we are told that shortly after the book has been revealed that Lebanon shall be turned into a fruitful field.

In ancient times, Lebanon was covered with giant cedars. They were cut down by Solomon to build his temple, by the Phoenicicaus to build boats and the Pharaohs to build their kingdoms. The area became virtually void of trees. Now dams have been built and citrus trees planted. Currently, it is known as the citrus belt, literally turning into a fruitful field.

Now we must ask ourselves; is there any other sealed book

which has come forth to fulfill the prophecy of Isaiah? If there is, it must have come forth before April 1958 when Lebanon was once again established as a fruitful field.

There is only one book that fulfills the prophecy of being a sealed book to come forth before the change in Lebanon. Only one book that was sealed and taken to a learned man who could not read it but was translated by an unlearned man. Only one book that fulfills the prophecy of Ezekiel and claims to be the stick of Joseph joined together with the stick of Judah prior to the gathering of Israel. Only one book that satisfies all of these things and claims to be the word of God to the ancient inhabitants of the Americas.

THAT BOOK IS THE BOOK OF MORMON! If it fulfills the prophecies of the prophets of God, it must be the word of God. If it is the word of God, it must be true and it must have been brought forth from a prophet of God. JOSEPH SMITH IS THE PROPHET OF GOD WHO BROUGHT FORTH THE BOOK OF MORMON! If Joseph Smith is a prophet of God, the church he established must be the church of God! THE CHURCH OF JESUS CHRIST OF LATTER-DAY SAINTS IS THE TRUE CHURCH OF THE LIVING GOD!

In verses 18-24 of Isaiah 29 we find that the book is here to bring us out of darkness and to teach us the doctrines of the kingdom.

Now for your assignment. When you get on your knees tonight, thank God for allowing you to belong to His true Church! Thank Him for allowing you to prepare for a mission where you can teach your brothers and sisters who have been spiritually deaf or blind that the gospel has been restored and is on the earth today. Thank Him for living prophets and that you came to the earth in the literal fulness of times!

I close the main portion of this book with my testimony

that God lives, Jesus is the Christ, the young boy Joseph Smith saw what he said he saw and he is the prophet of the restoration, we have a living prophet today and the Book of Mormon is indeed the word of God! What a blessing to know these things are completely true!

There is no message more important than the message you will teach. Now go forth to serve and teach with the power of God!

# CHAPTER 9

# IN CONCLUSION . . .

Now in conclusion, I want to leave you with just a couple of thoughts. You will probably find that you will not be nearly as excited to leave the mission field as you are to enter it. When you serve the people and learn to love them unconditionally, you find it hard to leave them. They will love you for the blessings you have made them aware of and the spirit they have felt when you were in their homes. They will always know you as the missionary who taught them or baptized them. You will have an eternal connection with them that cannot be broken.

One thing is certain; you will eventually be released from your mission. It will end! It is the same way with almost any calling you will receive in the church. If you are called . . . eventually you will be released.

When I teach my class, I bring a roll of film. I note to the students that there are twenty-four exposures in the film and tell them that it corresponds with the number of months they will be serving in the mission field. Then I talk to them about what they are going to leave on their "film." Once a day passes, it is gone forever and cannot be retrieved. No matter how much you might want to get it back, it is impossible. I begin to pull the film out of the roll, exposing it to the light, and continue to pull it out until it is all exposed. As I do, I continue to express to them the need to make sure that whatever is on their film is good. It must reflect hard work. It must show improvement and progress. It must be something that you can look back on without regret.

The time will come when you are boarding a plane, train or boat or some other mode of transportation to return to your home. As you look out the window you will think about how you did on your mission. You will probably ask yourself something like, "I wonder if I did all that I could have and should have on my mission?" As you seriously ponder that question or one similar to it one of two things will happen. You will either feel an empty, vacant feeling telling you that you really did not do all you could have, or you will have a wonderful feeling that is almost indescribable. It will be almost as though the arms of the Lord were encircling you and you will feel the warmth that assures you that you did do all you were supposed to do and your work has been accepted by God Himself! The things left on your "film" will be things that you can reflect on throughout your life that will bring you happiness and great joy.

I can almost assure you that whichever feeling you have at that time, it will resurface every time you hear the words 'mission' or 'missionary.' That can be either a great blessing or a dreadful curse. It's entirely up to you. I know returned missionaries who shudder whenever the word 'mission' is mentioned because what they left on their film was not what they really wanted. Sometimes they even have to leave the room and will not return until the topic has changed. How sad that their film causes them such discomfort. On the other hand, when others I know hear the word 'mission,' they feel blessed to have the feelings of peace and satisfaction envelop their entire soul. It is a sacred and personal experience that cannot fully be described.

Now please don't misunderstand me by feeling like if you make a single mistake in the mission field that you will forever feel bad about your entire mission. That is not what I am suggesting. What I am saying is that if you simply do all that you can to do your very best, including repenting of mistakes you make and going forward in the work, your mission will be a source of great comfort and peace to you throughout your entire life.

WORK HARD, VERY HARD, AND BE PERFECTLY OBEDIENT AND YOU WILL BE BLESSED! If you are disobedient, change your perspective and behavior, repent and try your very best to always be obedient. Joseph Smith said that if you work hard and are completely obedient, it will be as though every one you spoke with joined the church.

If you work hard, you will have more positive experiences than if you do not. Do you know some missionaries who seem to have many many stories about their missions? They tracted out the last house on the long street and found someone praying for them to come or some other miraculous event. These types of experiences come to those who are out working as hard as they can. You will never have the "last house" type of experience if you are always in your apartment doing nothing. Get out and work hard and you will be blessed with experiences that will bless your entire life.

Now I want you to think what you would do if the Lord Himself came to your house and gave you something. Let's say He gave you a small silver ball. What would you do with it? Would you throw it away? Would you put it in your dresser to be lost in the bottom of a drawer? Would you put it in your pocket and keep it with you? I hope that you would treat it with great respect and give it a special place of significance. I hope that it would be something that you would look at frequently and remember from whence it came. I hope that this gift would be extremely important to you!

The Lord will give you a gift every day of your mission. He will give you twenty-four hours! Don't throw them away! Give them the respect they deserve as a gift from God. Use them wisely. After all, whose time is it really?

Remember that you will be having a once-in-a-lifetime

experience serving a mission as a single adult. Cherish each moment and relish each second and savor the entire experience.

The gospel is completely true! The message you carry is of more import than anything available on earth. You have the opportunity to be an instrument in the hands of God. Decide to do it and do it well!

# ABOUT THE AUTHOR

Lyman Hinckley Rose was born in Salt Lake City, Utah, on September 4, 1958, to Ford Thomas Rose and Beulah Hinckley Rose. He served a mission in the Australia Sydney Spanish Mission serving from November 1977 through February 1980 (having received a three-month extension). Part of his service as a missionary was spent under the careful direction of Loren C. Dunn who was his first mission president. The last part of his mission was spent with Orson Wright as the president.

He graduated from Brigham Young University in April 1985 with a degree in business finance, and he owns his own business.

He has taught Missionary Preparation for nine years on both the stake and college institute level, and developed his own curriculum in an attempt to satisfy the needs of the students in the class.

He married the former Lesa Peterson on March 15, 1982. They have nine children and reside in Bountiful, Utah.

He has served in many positions in the Church, but his passion has always been missionary work. As a family the Roses enjoy family and outdoor activities.